"As a mom who has graduated two daughte[rs] ... [I can] say with confidence that living the kind of homeschooling—the kind of resting in God—that Sarah discusses has paid off enormously in our home. *Teaching from Rest* is an encouraging, humble, honest, and gentle book. It is a gem."

—Karen Edmisten, karenedmisten.com, author of *Deathbed Conversions*, *After Miscarriage*, *The Rosary*, and *Through the Year with Mary*

"*Teaching from Rest* will fill even the most frantic, overwhelmed homeschooling mom with a deep sense of peace."

—Jennifer Fulwiler, conversiondiary.com, author of *Something Other than God*

"In this book, Sarah helps us breathe deeply, focus on the children we have in front of us, and plunge back into our calling with renewed vision and passion. *Teaching from Rest* is about letting go of our anxiety without giving up on diligence. Yes, we can do it!"

—Mystie Winckler, simplyconvivial.com, author of *Paperless Home Organization*

"Sarah Mackenzie is winsome and wise, a real ally for teachers in the trenches. *Teaching from Rest* is profoundly helpful for home educators at any stage. It's been a blast of light in our family, and a rich resource for our homeschooling community."

—S.D. Smith, author of *The Green Ember* and *The Black Star of Kingston*

"This book offered me both spiritual and practical inspiration and the reminder that God's definition of success is not completion of a particular curriculum, but rather, faithfulness to what He's called me to."

—Trina Holden, trinaholden.com, author of *Your Real Food Journey*

"In *Teaching from Rest*, Sarah beautifully reminds us that we will never be able to give our children the 'perfect' education. Instead of crumbling under the weight of our attempts to do so, we can let the burdens fall off our tired backs."

—Jamie Martin, simplehomeschool.net, author of *Give Your Child the World*

"*Teaching from Rest* is a quarterly read for me because that's how often I need a shot in the arm—not just for spearheading my kids' education, but for parenting. This book does just that. Sarah reminds me that I'm made to do this job of sharing the journey with my children, pointing the way as I forge my own path of learning. Her words are balm in a desert that taunts us with a need to be perfect at all times. *Teaching from Rest* reminds me to take care of myself so that I can pour out that needed passion from true, inward authenticity."

—Tsh Oxenreider, author of *Notes from a Blue Bike: The Art of Living Intentionally in a Chaotic World* and founder of theArtofSimple.net

"Reading *Teaching from Rest* was truly transformational to our entire homeschool year! I'd been feeling weary and burnt out as a homeschool mom and Sarah's words breathed life into my tired bones and fresh inspiration into our days. The benefits and blessings we've reaped in our home since implementing Morning Time have been amazing. It's so wonderful to be starting the homeschool day with anticipation instead of dread and to have my kids eager to learn and begging for more. Thank you, thank you, Sarah! We are eternally grateful to you!"

—Crystal Paine, New York Times bestselling author of *Say Goodbye to Survival Mode*, founder of moneysavingmom.com

"Restful teaching is elusive to any mama, much less us type-A types. *Teaching from Rest* is the reminder I need that I am not in control, nor should I be. If I put my trust in [God] and lean not unto mine own understanding everything is going to be all right. That is why this one is required reading *at least* once a year."

—Pam Barnhill, edsnapshots.com, author of *Plan Your Year*

Teaching from Rest

A Homeschooler's Guide to
UNSHAKABLE PEACE

Sarah Mackenzie

Foreword by Dr. Christopher Perrin

Teaching from Rest:
A Homeschooler's Guide to Unshakable Peace
© Classical Academic Press, 2015
Version 2.0, new and revised edition
First Printed Edition

ISBN: 978-1-60051-287-2

Scripture quotations are from the Revised Standard Version of the Bible, copyright 2000 [2nd Catholic edition, 2006] by the Division of Christian Education of the National Council of the Churches of Christ in the United States of America. Used by permission. All rights reserved.

Cover by Rebecca James
Layout by Kiley Ann Bradbury

Classical Academic Press
2151 Market Street
Camp Hill, PA 17011

www.ClassicalAcademicPress.com

PGP.05.16

For Andy, who knows me best and loves me anyway.

Table of Contents

Foreword

Sarah Mackenzie writes that "curriculum isn't something we buy," but rather "something we teach." I think she is right. In fact, I know she is right. Of course, we do use the word "curriculum" to mean the published resources we use to . . . to what? Well, to teach mathematics, Latin, or history—that is, to teach our curriculum.

Let's get this straight. Our curriculum is the course that we travel. In Latin, *curriculum* means "a running" or "a racecourse." Figuratively it means one's career—one's life course. In the classical tradition, curriculum meant a course of training in the liberal arts and the great books. When we use the word "curriculum" to refer to Singapore or Saxon Math, we are extending the meaning of the word to cover the resources we use to teach our curriculum. Both uses of the word are legitimate; the trouble is we know one use of the word and have forgotten the other. So Sarah is right to break the spell of our amnesia and tell us that curriculum is not something we buy, but something we teach.

She brings this up because she knows that we have not only forgotten the meaning of the word, but with it have forgotten the aims of education. She knows that we are tempted to follow closely, even slavishly and with a great deal of anxiety, the specifications of a published resource (our "curriculum"). We cover material, we rush to keep up or catch up, and what is lost in the process is a love of mathematics and our perception of its truth, goodness, and beauty. We instead simply get through the book. Ah, yes, let's just get through it.

Sarah can write about this so well because she is a convert. There was a time (a matter of years, we suspect) in which she was that anxious educator and parent, checking off boxes, covering material, and getting through books. But now she is not the same. She still uses books and resources to teach her children, but those books serve her and her curriculum; she no longer serves them. She knows better, by knowing the primary meaning of "curriculum." She has recovered the aims of education and she has learned how to rest—even as a parent-educator. She now aims at the cultivation of wisdom, virtue, and eloquence in the souls of her children.

This is heartening to me, because I travel the country speaking about the *scholé*—restful learning—approach to education. Over the years, I have found that several homeschooling educators have resonated with this approach, recognizing it as wise and true and setting out to change. They have surpassed me. Sarah is one of these educators, one who did more than attend a few lectures and read a book or two. She has contemplated the tradition of restful learning and has implemented it with her children, blessing them in the process. Her blog posts at AmongstLovelyThings.com are evidence of this. Her conversation confirms it. This book proves it. She has learned something vital about cultivating the souls of her children, seeking their wisdom and virtue and keeping published resources in their esteemed place as helps and aids, which is to say, as published resources. She is the teacher of her children, along with the great books. Published resources help her. One result: She has more responsibility but also more peace.

I say this as someone who publishes such resources, and as someone who struggles to practice what I preach in regard to restful learning and resting generally. I have preached before I have practiced. Sarah has practiced and now preaches. We will all do well to hear her words and observe her life.

Christopher A. Perrin, PhD
Classical Academic Press

Preface

When I sit down to write, sometimes I don't really know what I'm going to say. I start anyway, and almost inevitably the words start coming and I have to try to keep up with them. As I write, I wonder about the woman who might be encouraged by my words—who may find just a small bit of hope in them. I wonder how they will bless her; I hope that they will reach her. And that is why it is especially humbling to realize that the message is actually meant for *me*.

Usually within the preface, the writer discusses why he or she is the right person to be writing the book. In this case, I'm telling you why I *shouldn't* be writing it. I did not see this book coming. The message within it came first as a blog series, and even then the words were given to me through my incessant pleading.

I write this book as the mother of six, three of my children under two—the smallest of them identical twin boys. It seems almost paradoxical that right now—when I am more sleep deprived than I've ever been in my life—I'm writing about rest. On the one hand, it makes no sense. On the other, it makes all the sense in the world. This book sprang from an insatiable thirst for the unshakable peace that God promises those who follow Him. I long to live from a place of rest, to teach and mother from peace rather than anxiety. I'm quite certain that God desires that for all of us—His beloved daughters called to the educating and raising up of little hearts and minds.

I am just like you. I homeschool my kids, wash dishes, pile laundry, trip over Legos, obsess over the curriculum, think too much about which book we should read next, about whether I am doing enough or doing any of it well enough. I worry. I falter. I cave in to my fears and fret about what the neighbors think. I refuse to let God have His way with my kids, our family, and our homeschool, and I cling ever tighter to my illusions of control.

It was Andrew Kern from the CiRCE Institute (CirceInstitute.org) who first alerted me to my anxiety-riddled ways. I was watching an interview of him on YouTube when he stopped me in my tracks. He said, "The most important thing a homeschooling mother can do is to teach from a state of rest."

At the time I was pregnant with twins. I had a child who was barely a year old, three older kids to teach, a home to run, and the idea sounded, well . . . absurd.

Right, I thought, *at this very minute there is dinner to cook, laundry spilling into the hallway, the toddler getting into the bathroom cupboards (again), one child having a meltdown over handwriting, another making paper dolls instead of doing math, and a third shooting Nerf darts at my head. All this and I got five hours of (interrupted) sleep last night because the baby has an ear infection.*

I didn't understand what he meant by "rest."

He didn't mean teach your calm children in a calm manner on a calm afternoon. He didn't even mean teach on a full night's sleep (thank goodness). He meant that we ought to enter into God's rest and then serve Him wholeheartedly—not out of anxiety, but out of love and trust.

Over the course of the next year, I swallowed whole anything I could find about rest. I scoured the Internet and the Bible and every book that fell across my way. In the process, I discovered the work of Dr. Christopher Perrin from Classical Academic Press, who was also talking about restful teaching and learning—about *scholé*. Dr. Perrin was influential in my understanding of slow, sane education. My desire to teach my children from peace grew and grew. You can view Dr. Perrin's video on *scholé* at ClassicalAcademicPress.com and learn about homeschooling groups pursuing "restful learning" at ScholeGroups.com.

I would be remiss not to thank Andrew Kern and Dr. Perrin for their influence on my own personal state of rest. To Rebecca James—

thank you for believing in this project and in my ability to tackle it. Your confidence and encouragement helped me keep on.

I owe a debt of gratitude to my beautiful friends Pamela Barnhill and Mystie Winckler, who believed in this project and offered endless help and counsel from the moment it was just a vague idea. Thanks also to Elizabeth Foss, Angela Fredericks, Meghan Kunzl, Rosalie Nourse, Sheila Rahn, and Natalie Schroeder. You have been to me what Mary was to Elizabeth in her day of need. The insight and practical help you gave was invaluable. I thank God every time I remember you.

> We ought to enter into God's rest and then serve Him wholeheartedly—not out of anxiety, but out of love and trust.

To Andy and my beautiful big kids: thank you for putting up with the madness. For letting me shriek with glee when the words came to me like a rush, and for giving me space to hone them when they trickled out with much time and effort. Your support of my labors has meant the world to me. I hope all that time I disappeared to a coffee shop to write this book will be redeemed through His grace. I do everything for you . . . but sometimes I forget to tell you that.

For the readers of my blog, *Amongst Lovely Things*: All I have for you is heartfelt thanks. Your words of confidence and admonition spurred me on. You inspire and challenge me every day. The community we have built together brings me great hope and lifts me up when the days feel heavy.

Here is the bare truth: Not an hour passes without the enormity of the task I have taken on bringing me to my knees. This work of homeschooling and raising hearts and souls and bodies is hard. It is more than I can do in my own strength. Even so, more than anything else, I desire to teach and mother in a way that pleases God. Some days that feels like feeding the five thousand. But He is not asking me to feed the five thousand; He just wants me to bring my basket of loaves and fish and lay them at His feet.

I have no business whatsoever sounding like someone who has this figured out. I'm writing this book anyway because the message keeps rattling around in my heart and I won't be able to shake it free until I learn to embrace it: *Our hearts are restless until they rest in You, O Lord.*[1]

This work of homeschooling and raising hearts and souls and bodies is hard. It is more than I can do in my own strength.

1. Augustine, *Confessions*, trans. R.S. Pine-Coffin (New York: Penguin, 1983), book 1, n.p.

Preface

Introduction:
I Shouldn't Have
Written This Book

In the book of Philippians we are told to be anxious over nothing, yet we are anxious over everything.

> Have no anxiety about anything, but in everything by prayer and supplication with thanksgiving let your requests be made known to God. And the peace of God, which passes all understanding, will keep your hearts and your minds in Christ Jesus. (Philippians 4:6–7)

We worry that our students will be "behind," that they won't score well on the SAT, get into a good college, or read enough of the Great Books. Our souls are restless, anxiously wondering if something else out there might be just a little bit better—if maybe there is another way or another curriculum that might prove to be superior to what we are doing now. We choose anxiety as our guide instead of humbly submitting to God and letting Him guide us.

We all know the story of Mary and Martha, I'm sure (see Luke 10:38–42). Jesus was staying at their house, and Martha, anxious to please Him and make Him comfortable, was bustling about—doing and doing and doing. Her sister, Mary, was sitting at the Lord's feet, listening attentively, beholding, soaking in.

We can picture Martha in her frustration with her sister, right? "Don't just sit there! Do something!" And yet the Lord gently admonishes Martha's busyness. Mary, after all, has chosen the needful thing. The contemplative way. The being and becoming over the doing and the checking off. I can almost hear him inverting the message to me—turning my obsession with productivity on its head: "Don't just do something; sit here."

As homeschooling moms, we are anxious and troubled about many things; one thing is needful. If we choose the good portion, it will not be taken from us.

We are called to work. That part we have down, more or less. We home-schooling mothers are quite adept at spinning our wheels, working dawn to dusk to make sure our children have everything they need. We toil tirelessly to create lesson plans and assemble curriculum that will ensure our children know everything they need to know before they fly our coop.

We worry. We fret. We know, deep down in the core of our being, that we are not enough. That what we offer is a pittance compared to the task before us. We feel small and insignificant because we *are* small and insignificant.

> The heart of this book is about remembering what our true task really is, and then throwing ourselves in completely. Giving our all. The raising of children, the teaching of truth, the sharing of life, the nourishing of imagination, and the cultivating of wisdom — these are all His anyway; we are merely His servants.

In the midst of all the doing, we forget the needful thing. We may sit at His feet; we may begin our day with prayer, Bible reading, and supplication, but is our teaching and mothering transformed by it? Do we really trust Him? Do we live each day from a state of rest?

God doesn't call us to this work and then turn away to tend to other, more important matters. He promises to stay with us, to lead us, to carry us. He assures us that if we rely on Him alone, then He will provide all that we need. What that means on a practical level is that we have to stop fretting over every little detail. We need to stop comparing. We've got to drop the self-inflated view that *we* are the be-all and end-all of whether the education we are offering our children is going to be as successful as we hope it is.

After all, our job is not to be successful—success itself is entirely beside the point. It's faithfulness that He wants. God is good! He isn't going to let us pour out our hearts for our children only to be left choking on the dust of our mistakes.

Can we seek Him first? Can we live and teach from a state of rest? My prayer is that we will. But we must approach the Holy Spirit every single day, asking Him to lead us and to quiet our anxious souls so that we can really bless our children—not with shiny curriculum or perfect lesson plans, but rather with purposeful, restful spirits.

The true aim of education is to order a child's affections—to teach him to love what he ought and hate what he ought. Our greatest task, then, is to put living ideas in front of our children like a feast. We have been charged to cultivate the souls of our children, to nourish them in truth, goodness, and beauty, to raise them up in wisdom and eloquence. It is to those ends that we labor.

We toil because we long to be like the man in Psalm 1, who is "like a tree planted by streams of water, that yields its fruit in its season, and its leaf does not wither. In all that he does, he prospers" (1:3).

The heart of this book is about remembering what our true task really is, and then throwing ourselves in completely. Giving our all. The raising of children, the teaching of truth, the sharing of life, the nourishing of imagination, and the cultivating of wisdom: These are all His anyway; we are merely His servants.

The first edition of this book was available as an e-book only. After receiving feedback from the readers of the e-book, I put much thought and care into revisions for this second edition. The material has been reorganized and added to, and it is my utmost prayer that these changes bless and encourage you. Teaching from rest is a lifelong journey. I'm not sure we ever really arrive, but the way we encourage and build each other up along the way has the ability to shape our lives and the lives of our children for eternity.

I'm so glad to hook arms with you for this journey—may God's most abundant blessings be yours now and always.

Before You Read This Book

You may want to get your hands on the companion set of *Teaching from Rest*—it contains a printable journal and a set of audio files. The companion journal will help you work through the principles discussed in these pages. You can print it out and use the commonplace area to copy out any passages or quotes that you don't want to forget. The journal prompts included will help you dig out ideas and live them out in your home and heart.

The audio companion is a collection of recorded conversations between myself and the educator-mentors whom I respect most. This is delivered as a set of MP3 downloads. It includes:

- *Teach from a State of What?!*
  with Andrew Kern

- *Scholé: Changing the Way We Think about School*
  with Dr. Christopher Perrin

- *Let's Get Real: Mothering from a State of Rest*
  with Brandy Vencel

- *If I Knew Then What I Know Now*
  with Cindy Rollins

You will find all of the companion materials at ClassicalAcademicPress.com.

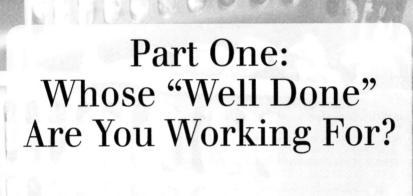

Part One: Whose "Well Done" Are You Working For?

The real problem of the Christian life comes where people do not usually look for it. It comes the very moment you wake up each morning. All your wishes and hopes for the day rush at you like wild animals. And the first job each morning consists simply in shoving them all back; in listening to that other voice, taking that other point of view, letting that other larger, stronger, quieter life come flowing in. And so on, all day. Standing back from all your natural fussings and frettings; coming in and out of the wind.

—C.S. Lewis, *Mere Christianity*

The Cake under the Couch

> Everything that happens each day in the little universe of our work and our family, in the circle of our friends and acquaintances, can and must help us to find God's providence. Fulfillment of the divine will and the knowledge that it is being done is a source of serenity and gratitude.
>
> —Francis Fernandez, *In Conversation with God*

Rest begins with acceptance. Or, perhaps more accurately, with surrender. There will always be more you can do. You will never complete your tasks entirely, because just on the horizon is tomorrow, and tomorrow the to-do list starts anew. It is so exhausting—sometimes even demoralizing—to realize that our work in raising up and teaching our children is never really done. But we must remember that we were never intended to finish it.

In *Holiness for Housewives and Other Working Women*, Hubert Van Zeller tells us, "The whole business of serving God becomes simply a matter of adjusting yourself to the pressures of existing conditions. . . . This is the first lesson for the Christian wife and mother today: to let go of what may once have been—and under other circumstances might now be—a recollected self, and take on, with both hands, the plan of God."[1]

> Rest begins with acceptance. Or, perhaps more accurately, with surrender.

What are those existing conditions? What is keeping you from speeding through the reading curriculum, flying through the math book, checking off the lesson plans, and maximizing efficiency? Usually the answer is: people. Can you hit the pause button on your frustration long enough to realize that people rank infinitely higher than anything else on the list? Have you considered that God may have scooted these people into view for the very purpose of slowing you down?

---

1. Hubert Van Zeller, *Holiness for Housewives and Other Working Women* (Manchester, NH: Sophia Institute Press, 1997), 14–15.

When a person interrupts what you are doing, you [ought to] recognize a representative of Christ. When the dog is seen getting under the sofa with tonight's dessert, you at once assume that God wants you to put aside the half hour you have been looking forward to (which you meant to spend with a book in church or doing the stations of the Cross) to make another dessert.[2]

Whatever is getting in the way of your plan for the day—the toddler's tantrum, the messy bedroom, the sticky juice leaking all over the fridge and into the cracks of the drawers, the frustrated child, the irritable husband, the car that won't start, the cake the dog dragged under the couch . . . whatever that intrusion into your grand plan for the day is, it's also an opportunity to enter into rest. C.S. Lewis once observed:

> The great thing, if one can, is to stop regarding all the unpleasant things as interruptions of one's "own," or "real" life. The truth is of course that what one calls the interruptions are precisely one's real life—the life God is sending one day by day; what one calls one's "real life" is a phantom of one's own imagination.[3]

We can't really rest in God's care until we trust that He *will* indeed care for us. And that means I can't teach from rest unless I trust Him with my kids' education too. I am not meant to take on this task of teaching and raising my children in my own strength, and neither are you. We are, however, meant to recognize every facet of our day as coming from the hand of God. It all passes through His fingers first, and He uses it to make sure that we lean hard on Him. QUESTION OF THE DAY

Surrender your idea of what the ideal homeschool day is supposed to look like and take on, with both hands, the day that it *is*. Rest begins with acceptance, with surrender. Can we accept what He is sending today?

---

2. Van Zeller, *Holiness for Housewives*, 31.
3. C.S. Lewis, *Letters of C.S. Lewis*, ed. W.H. Lewis (New York: Mariner Books, 2003), 499.

Rest Is Not Ease

It's important to remember that rest is not ease. This isn't idealism. It isn't simple and peaceful in the sense of being easy or gentle. Teaching from rest is meaningful learning and growth—but without the anxiety and frenzy so common in our day. Contrary to what you might think at first when you hear "teaching from rest," teaching from rest will take diligence, attention, and a lot of hard work.

Unshakable peace does not come from getting through a certain amount of material over a specified amount of time, but it also doesn't come from throwing in the towel and giving in when things get hard. Peace comes from recognizing that our real task is to wake up each day and get our marching orders from God. It comes from diligence to the work He hands us, but diligence infused with faith, with resting in God's promises to guide and bless us.

Teaching from rest doesn't mean that we let our children dictate the curriculum, that we ignore timetables altogether and decide we don't care if our children ever get into college or pass their exams. *Rest is trusting that God's got this, even if I'm a mess, even if I'm not enough, even if I mess up every day. Because I do.*

We have this desire to give our kids what we call an academically "rigorous" education. Andrew Kern and Christopher Perrin both taught me a bit about that. In my conversations with them for the audio companion to this book (available at teachingfromrest.com), I asked them how we could pursue a rigorous education while retaining a sense of rest. What I didn't realize at the time was that the word "rigor" comes from the Latin *rigor, rigoris*, which means "numbness, stiffness, hardness, firmness, roughness, rudeness." *Rigor mortis* literally means "the stiffness of death," which I think we can all agree is not the goal of homeschooling our children!

Don't aim for a rigorous education, Kern and Perrin both told me. *If we are aiming to order our children's affections, learn to love what is lovely, join in the great conversation, and cultivate a soul so that the person is ready in every sense of the word to take on the challenges around the corner and on the other side of the college entrance exams; work toward "diligence" instead.*

"Diligence" comes from the Latin *diligere*, which means to "single out, value highly, esteem, prize, love; aspire to, take delight in, appreciate." What we are really aiming for in giving our children a rigorous education is not just doing hard things, but cultivating a habit of focused attention. The word "student" comes from the Latin *studium*, meaning "zeal, affection, eagerness." A diligent student, then, takes delight, eagerly and with great zeal, in what he loves.

Through a restful diligence we work at the right things in the right way at the right time—as God gives us that wisdom. We are diligent about the things we love, and we can love what must be done because we have been blessed and loved by a God who even enables us to love our enemies. Surely if we can love our enemies, then we can love the laundry, or Latin, or math studies. When we are diligent, even our mundane daily tasks can be offered up to God as gifts of love and sacrifice.

As Laura Ingalls Wilder reminds us, "The true way to live is to enjoy every moment as it passes, and surely it is in the everyday things around us that the beauty of life lies."[4]

So what does this mean as I am entrenched in my actual day? What happens when my child throws down her pencil and her eyes well up with tears because she just doesn't get the math lesson today? (This happens in my home quite a bit!)

When I focus on being diligent rather than rigorous, my measure for success is not, "Did I check off lesson 97 today?" I *am* going to want to check off lesson 97 at some point. But if I can't do it today because my child is not achieving understanding, I don't need to fret and worry and wring my hands. I'm not tempted to push her through to the next lesson because we must! keep! up!, and I certainly don't put the math book on the shelf and shrug it off either.

---

4. Laura Ingalls Wilder, *Laura Ingalls Wilder: Farm Journalist: Writings from the Ozarks*, ed. Stephen W. Hines (Columbia: University of Missouri, 2007), 88.

When my child does not understand a math lesson, it should not disturb my state of peace. After all, God intends that study and work involve challenges that we face and overcome, so we expect difficulties from time to time when teaching our children. Now it's time to troubleshoot, problem-solve, and come alongside her. When she doesn't understand the day's lesson, it isn't a setback; it's just God showing us our marching orders for the day. My child doesn't need me to fret and fear; she needs me to love and guide her with grace.

Teaching from rest means we don't panic when things don't go according to our plan—in fact, we plan for plans not always to work well. When I take on the challenge of this day with both hands and trust that we are right where He wants us, that's when I experience, unshakable peace. Not when the work is all done, the lessons all checked off, the SAT aced, and my child sent successfully to college, proving that I did my job well.

In fact, unshakable peace is not tied to my success at all. It's tied to faithfulness. We rest in knowing that if our children grow up to ask us why we did what we did—why we focused on cultivating wonder and curiosity, on learning hard things such as Latin and algebra, why we didn't fill up our days but focused on living well and gazing on Him—we can answer them with confidence.

In his landmark book *Orthodoxy*, G.K. Chesterton tells us that secular culture is made up of virtues run wild, and we see this tendency clearly when it comes to our teaching.[5] If studiousness is a virtue worth cultivating, I find that I am drawn toward vice on either side of it. On the one hand, I am drawn to steamroll over my kids, to lord over them with checklists and grade levels without regard to their nature as unique persons made in the image of God. On the other, I am drawn to negligence or carelessness. I comfort myself with adages about children learning all the time and, hoping that my child will encounter an idea

---

5. G.K. Chesterton, *Orthodoxy* (Lexington, KY: Ortho Publishing, 2014).

for himself without my interference, fail to form my student's affections out of fear that such work is coercion or manipulation.

Rest is the virtue between negligence and anxiety, but many of the homeschooling moms I have met, myself included, find themselves more likely to fall prey to one camp or the other. When we are weak in virtue, we inch toward vice. A curriculum that leaves no room for the soul to breathe will suffocate, but so will the absence of purposeful and intentional teaching. If we are doing our children a great disservice by shuttling them through a set of books and plans without consideration for their souls, we are doing them an equal disservice by ignoring their formation and leaving our children to form themselves.

Let's really think about this. If our children are images of God (and they are), then we aren't meeting their needs or tending to their real nature when we swing like a pendulum to either the vice of anxiety or the vice of negligence.

I spent some of my early homeschooling years parked in an overly relaxed mode of teaching. It wasn't laziness, exactly—I went in quite intentionally and thought it to be a great gift to my students to allow them to bloom on their own terms. What I found, however, was that the nature of my children was not nurtured by my best intentions. My neglect in their formation reaped exactly what one might expect—laziness, carelessness, and a self-centered view of learning. I thought I was meeting my kids where they were. I wrongly figured that if wisdom began with wonder, then I as a teacher ought to step out of the way completely. In an effort not to stand between my student and his learning, I failed to build a bridge at all between the child in front of me and the man God intended him to become.

The Greek historian Plutarch once wrote, "The mind is not a vessel that needs filling, but wood that needs igniting."[6]

---

6. Plutarch, "On Listening," in *Essays*, trans. Robin H. Waterfield, ed. Ian Kidd (London: Penguin Classics, 1993), 50.

Modern translations of Plutarch's maxim tell us that education is not the filling of a bucket, but the lighting of a fire, but we must remember that a fire does indeed need to be lit and then stoked, or else it will burn out.

Teaching from rest is not the absence of work or the abdication of our responsibility to form and shape our students. In Luke 6:40 we learn that a student, fully formed, will become like his teacher. Clearly, then, a teacher cannot form and train a student by staying in the shadows.

Rest, therefore, is not the absence of work or a failure to consider and carry out a plan. It is work and leisure, properly ordered. It is doing the right thing at the right time, realizing that our task is to hear God's call and follow His commands, and then to trust that God will be God—to be at rest even while at work.

Much of our anxiety in homeschooling could be sidestepped by simply acknowledging who we are trying to please. It sounds simplistic, but consider that your day—what you prioritize, what you don't—will likely look different depending on whether you are doing it all for His pleasure, or doing it all (or only some of it) to please Grandma, the neighbor, or anyone else... *or self.*

Who am I trying to impress, anyway? What ends up on my list of essentials may not look remarkable to the state or to anyone else, but I just have to keep reminding myself: That doesn't matter. I cannot serve two masters, and neither can you. Whose "well done" are you working for?

Why Your Daily Grind Is Holy Ground

Most of my own frustration comes from forgetting what my real task is in the first place. He's called me to be faithful, yet I'm determined to be successful. For example, I have a tendency to think (and teach) as though I have been charged with the task of successfully raising lifelong learners. I judge my success or failure in my teaching either by the tools my child has in his academic toolbox at the end of a school year, or by whether she still enjoys school, pursues knowledge, and chooses to read stacks of high-quality books in her free time.

What I forget is that whether or not she does any of these things is not an effective measuring stick for whether I've been doing my job. God is not demanding I be successful on my own. He's calling me to be faithful and to trust Him for the results, which may not look like what I was expecting. Success in God's eyes may not always look like the success we were seeking, but if we are faithful, we will know His peace and rest in our studies and efforts. What more success could we want?

Faithfulness is showing up every day to do the work He has called us to. Whether or not things turn out in the end as I'm hoping they will (for my children to have a strong faith, humble and compassionate hearts, a love for learning, and an academic skill set that helps them seek out knowledge and truth every day and everywhere) is not actually within my span of control. It's not my assigned task. He isn't asking me to succeed on the world's terms. He's asking me to faithfully do the work.

Consider St. Monica, the devoted mother of St. Augustine of Hippo. Despite his mother's prayerful and devoted care, Augustine grew to be a wild and ruthless young man—throwing himself into sin with reckless abandon. He broke his mother's heart and turned against the faith she had tried to instill in him at every turn.

Her long-suffering prayers were not laid waste. Her son did eventually convert and even became a doctor of the Church—arguably the most influential church father of all time. Yet if Monica had judged the success or failure of her mothering based on her son's behavior at age twenty, she would have considered herself a failure.

Do you see? We must drop the self-inflated view that we are the be-all and end-all of whether the education we offer our children is going to work out. We are too quick to feel both the successes and the failures of our job as homeschoolers. Our kids test well on the SAT and we pat ourselves on the back. They are miserable writers and we scourge ourselves for failing them. But He never demands that we produce prodigies or achieve what the world would recognize as excellence. Rather, He asks us to live excellently—that is, to live in simple, obedient faith and trust. He asks us to faithfully commit every day to Him and then to do that day's tasks well. He's in charge of the results.

The success we seek is not the same success that the world seeks. All true education begins in wonder and ends in wisdom—as Kevin Clark and Ravi Scott Jain so eloquently describe in *The Liberal Arts Tradition*.[7]

That writing assignment on the plan today? Do it well. That math lesson that your child struggles over? Sit down next to him, and do one problem at a time, slowly and carefully. Smile a lot. Lavish him with love. Because whether or not he becomes an excellent writer or a proficient mathematician is not your business to worry over. Your business is that single assignment today and loving him through it.

We all long to hear, "Well done, good and faithful servant; you have been faithful over a little, I will set you over much; enter into the joy of your master" (Matthew 25:21, 23). Our task is to love God with all of

---

7. Kevin Clark and Ravi Scott Jain, *The Liberal Arts Tradition: A Philosophy of Christian Classical Education* (Camp Hill, PA: Classical Academic Press, 2013).

our heart, mind, soul, and strength, and to do it in front of and with our kids (see Deuteronomy 6:5; Matthew 22:37). To do it when we rise up and when we walk along the way (see Deuteronomy 6:7). Each and every one of those little moments are part of something beautiful you are making for God—you are building a cathedral.

Build a Cathedral, Cultivate a Garden

> Once you have realized you are in the presence of God, cast yourself down with deep reverence before him and acknowledge your unworthiness to appear in his majestic presence, asking for all the graces you need to serve him well, knowing that in his goodness he longs to grant them to you.
>
> —St. Frances de Sales

> Education is an atmosphere, a discipline, and a life.
>
> —Charlotte Mason, *A Philosophy of Education*

It is easy to forget that teaching is holy work. The building up of the intellect—teaching children to really think—does not happen by the might of human reason, but rather by the grace of God. On an ordinary day, you and I likely have a set of tasks we've scheduled for our kids. But it's more than math. It's more than history. It is the building up of our children's minds and hearts, and we can only do that if we realize that this is how we thank Him for the graces He so lavishly pours upon us.

I tend to get lost in the details of large-family life when I'm right in the midst of it. It takes a certain fortitude, after all, to look at a pile of dishes and see it as the makings of a cathedral. The daily mundane is holy ground because the ordinary tasks of a monotonous Monday are where we meet our Maker.

The builders of medieval cathedrals knew what it meant to work their entire lives to please God without ever expecting to see their work completed. Many cathedrals would take more than a hundred years to build—more than the span of a man's lifetime. I once heard a story of an artisan who worked tirelessly for many years to carve a beautiful bird into the wood of a portion of the cathedral that would be covered up. When someone asked why he was working so hard on something that no one would see, he replied, "Because God sees."

God sees your little wooden bird too. Just as the artisans and carpenters of old built beautiful cathedrals for the glory of God, so do you. Yes, you—you who work tirelessly day after day over a geography lesson, a math test, a laundry pile, a kitchen sink. Those are the moments wherein you build cathedrals for God.

We are doing the small, difficult tasks day by day, one stone at a time. The cathedral builders toiled for years of their lives without knowing whether they would see the finished cathedral—the holy place to which they had given their lives. A homeschooling mother acts on similar faith—adding one small brick at a time—wondering if it makes a difference, if anyone will ever notice, if those small quotidian tasks will ever add up in a meaningful way.

At the end of our lives, He is going to look into our hearts. What is it He will find there, I wonder? Will He find that we used the geography lesson, the dreaded math test, the teetering laundry pile, and the boiling-over pot of soup to draw closer to Him? Did we use these gifts to teach our children to lift their eyes heavenward? Were the tedious details of a homeschooling day offered up as a way for us to love Him, or were they merely gotten through, checked off, and accomplished? Did we even realize that every Monday, every Thursday, every ordinary day, we were standing on holy ground, building a cathedral far more glorious than what we could dream up on our own?

No task is too trivial, no assignment too small. Educating our children is an offering of love we make to the God who was so gracious to bestow them upon us in the first place. Every moment of the daily grind in raising and teaching and loving on them is hallowed, because we do it for Him and because there would be no point of doing it without Him.

So what does that look like in the context of an actual day? That is the question I hear most often in regard to teaching from rest—and indeed, it is one I ask repeatedly myself. If we are called to teach from rest, yet our families and homeschools all look slightly different, where is the common ground? How does God's rest manifest on a Tuesday afternoon within the walls of my ordinary, slightly chaotic home?

Rest looks like stewardship. Consider a garden—a raised bed right outside your kitchen window, perhaps. The Master Gardener has charged you to plant it with seeds, to cultivate the soil, to tend to the plants and help them to flourish. He did not throw some seeds at you and tell you that you were responsible for the miracle of turning them to ripe, plump vegetables. He placed the seeds into your palm, patted your fist lovingly, and asked you to tend them well. To steward them. To help them grow.

Remember your place, then. You cannot make the plants grow or bear fruit. You can only plant the seeds. You can water them, and steward them. You can cultivate the soil (education is an atmosphere!), thin them (a discipline!), and water them (a life!). It is only by our cooperation with the grace of God and the laws of nature that the seed becomes a plant and bears fruit. We don't need to have anxiety about when the plant will grow, about how quickly it will come to fruition—our part is to steward it and do what we can to make sure it has the ability to grow rightly.

We only receive grace for reality. God does not bestow grace on us for all of the things that we think might go wrong in the future—for the possibility that a child will fail the SAT, will not have the tools he needs for a college education or a bright future, or even, more immediately, for the likelihood that this math lesson will end in tears.

No, we are given grace for right this moment—for reality. We must operate within that reality and within the laws of nature as we steward our garden. We can fret all we want that God will not turn our tomato seeds into cucumbers, but to what end?

Be encouraged. Those seeds our Lord has tucked into your hand can bear great fruit in the kingdom of God—but it takes something from you. It takes a reliance on providence, a commitment to faithful stewardship, and a state of restful trust. Cultivate your garden.

Bring Your Basket

> Come to me, all who labor and are heavy laden, and I will give you rest. Take my yoke upon you, and learn from me; for I am gentle and lowly in heart, and you will find rest for your souls. For my yoke is easy, and my burden is light. (Matthew 11:28-30)

Is there a part of you that is a bit cynical about that verse? Does the yoke feel easy and the burden light? It doesn't to me. Most days I wake up and can barely stagger out of bed under the heft of my load.

Just like the disciples, I see this huge throng of people to feed—this seeming impossibility. The shaping of souls and raising of children, the mopping of floors, washing of dishes, bandaging of scraped knees and hearts and worries, the teaching and admonishing and loving and doling out of myself. It's all too much. There are six children in this home; there is one of me. I fall to my knees and I cry out to God. We're a throng of hungry people in the desert, and I'm supposed to feed them. On an ordinary Monday, I am in need of a miracle of biblical proportions.

It isn't that I have nothing, exactly. I have my little basket. I can read aloud pretty well. I'm good at organizing things on paper. I can make a decent pot of chili and I know how to push a vacuum. I love my children with all of my being and I have a real desire to watch them grow to love and serve Him. I don't really have any idea how I'm supposed to tackle everything ahead of me in this day, this year, this decade when that's all I've got. It's just a couple loaves of bread and a few fish.

Apparently, that's all He needs.

We are weary because we forget about grace. We act as though God's showing up is the miracle. But guess what? God's showing up is the given. Grace is a fact.

If you are being asked to feed a multitude with a tiny basket of loaves and fish, then bring your basket. He starts with that. Just like the crowd in the wilderness, which had been faithfully following Jesus for days, sitting at His feet, savoring His words, seeking Him earnestly, we do the same. We bring our basket—whatever talents, skills, abilities we have—and we seek Him with everything we are. He works the miracle.

> We should count on the five loaves and the two fishes. By themselves they won't make much of a meal for so many hungry people at the end of a long day, but they nevertheless play an indispensable part in the working of the miracle.[8]

Remember your true task. Surrender everything. Bring your loaves and your fish, even if you think them completely insufficient. They are insufficient. You are insufficient. But His grace is not. God is not limited by objective reality. His yoke is easy and His burden light.

It All Starts with Prayer

I suspect that all of our attempts to teach from a state of rest are futile unless prayer is the cornerstone. We've got to start there. An

---

8. Francis Fernandez, *In Conversation with God*, vol. 4 (London, Scepter, 2010), 299.

indispensable part of bringing our basket, prayer puts aside "doing" in favor of "being" and "becoming": being in His presence and becoming more like Him.

When we begin the day by offering it up to God, we acknowledge that no matter what comes our way, we are doing it all for His pleasure. We remind ourselves that He is who He says He is, and that nothing matters except pleasing Him. Whether or not our children bicker all day, whether or not we get through the lesson plans, whether or not we barely hang on while everything falls apart around us—none of it matters except that we offer it up to God. And then all of it matters, but in a whole new light.

It's important that we not allow ourselves to be intimidated by prayer. Rather than worry about how long we pray or how many times we have to bring our minds back from wandering, we show up, sit at the foot of the cross, and put aside our own wills in order to give ourselves completely to His will.

Aspirations

An aspiration is a short prayer sent up throughout the day. Aspirations are excellent for ordering our minds toward Christ when we're in the thick of things. Use them when you begin to feel your day spinning out of orbit and then keep sending them up as you muddle through. You can use any short prayer or Scripture—just commit it to memory and start saying it throughout the day.

Here are a few to get you started:

O Lord Jesus Christ, Son of God, have mercy on me, a sinner.

Jesus, my God, I love Thee above all things.

Jesus, I trust in You.

My God and my all.

My Lord and my God!

God, come to my assistance. Lord, make haste to help me. (*This one is my personal favorite*)

O Lord, increase my faith.

Thou art the Christ, the Son of the living God.

Daily prayer doesn't have to be a long, drawn-out ritual. During some seasons of our lives, it simply *can't* be a long, drawn-out ritual. It can happen while you take your shower and get dressed for the day, while you prepare breakfast, or while you nurse the baby first thing in the morning. The key is that it happens every day.

Prayer before Study

Consider printing the *Ante Studium* ("before study") of St. Thomas Aquinas and praying it as a family at breakfast. Taking a few minutes to pray this together may help everyone—teacher and students both— approach the day mindful of the eternal nature each ordinary home-school day presents.

> Ineffable Creator,
> Who, from the treasures of Your wisdom,
> have established three hierarchies of angels,
> have arrayed them in marvelous order
> above the fiery heavens,
> and have marshaled the regions
> of the universe with such artful skill,
>
> You are proclaimed
> the true font of light and wisdom,
> and the primal origin
> raised high beyond all things.
>
> Pour forth a ray of Your brightness
> into the darkened places of my mind;
> disperse from my soul

the twofold darkness
into which I was born:
sin and ignorance.

You make eloquent the tongues of infants.
Refine my speech
and pour forth upon my lips
The goodness of Your blessing.

Grant to me
keenness of mind,
capacity to remember,
skill in learning,
subtlety to interpret,
and eloquence in speech.

May You
guide the beginning of my work,
direct its progress,
and bring it to completion.

You Who are true God and true Man,
who live and reign, world without end.

Amen.[9]

Before we attempt to live a day well, teach our children, or tackle our to-dos, *first* we put the whole thing at His feet. We beg God to use us to fulfill His purpose, and then we see that every frustration in the day ahead is an answer to that very prayer.

---

9. Thomas Aquinas, "Prayer Before Study," Aquinas College, last modified April 29, 2013, http://www.aquinascollege.edu/prayer-before-study-exams-spring-2013/.

We recognize all the small moments throughout our day for
what they are—the makings of a cathedral of timeless beauty,
the planting of seeds that will bear fruit in their season.

Part Two: Curriculum Is Not Something You Buy

Never be in a hurry; do everything quietly and in a calm spirit. Do not lose your inner peace for anything whatsoever, even if your whole world seems upset.

—St. Frances de Sales

How to Simplify the Curriculum

What if we've got it all wrong? What if it doesn't matter which books we use, which history projects we take on, or how many lessons of math we accomplish in a year?

Homeschoolers spend an inordinate amount of time thinking about "curriculum," but what if when we compare spelling programs and choose math books, we aren't really talking about curriculum at all? Curriculum isn't something we buy. It's something we teach. Something we embody. Something we love. It is the form and content of our children's learning experiences.

If we started thinking about "school" in terms of encountering certain ideas and mastering certain skills rather than finishing a particular book or "covering" material, we would free ourselves to learn far more than we can by binding ourselves to a set published resource. Of course we will use such resources to reach our goals, but the resource will be our servant, not our master.

Most of the homeschoolers I know take choosing published resources very seriously. This is a good thing. Our published resources help us cultivate wisdom, virtue, and eloquence in our students. If our books are beautiful and carefully chosen, then they will assist us in teaching our children to love that which is lovely. They will go a long way toward forming our students' affections and orienting them toward the good, true, and beautiful.

However, how we interact with our children while using the material matters far more than whether or not we get through it. Instead of focusing on what we need to cover in any given year, it may be helpful to think about what we might uncover and master. After all, if our eyes are so fixed on the finish line that we miss the experience entirely, what have we really gained for our labors? • FRUSTRATED? STOP AND GO BACK LATER

Which would you value more: to know that your child has turned the pages through four of Shakespeare's plays this year, or to watch him

• GOD, PLEASE CULTIVATE A LOVE OF LEARNING IN OUR HOME

QUALITY VS. QUANTITY

fall in love with *Henry V*? To have an impressive reading list with check marks next to every title, or to dive into a few carefully chosen stories that nurture the heart, mind, and soul? Does it really matter if your child has finished every math problem in the book by the end of May? Or will it make your heart sing if he has encountered the distributive property in such a way that he can see it a mile away, can wonder with awe at it, can use it with ease, and relish its exactitude?

How you teach is just as important as *what* you teach. What does your pacing or your lesson say to your student? When your student experiences learning as diving in, talking about great ideas, and getting lost in the beauty and truth of a classic or an

algebra problem that works out just perfectly (as it always does)—when learning is more a liturgy of love than a daily slog—only then will he realize his full potential as a student.

Some of the best learning happens when a child encounters an idea for himself. We are responsible for presenting the feast, but we can't always predict when or how that encounter will happen. It likely won't be as tidy and quantifiable as we think it should be.

Here's a hard truth we might as well get used to: Much of the best learning cannot be proven, measured, or easily demonstrated. The kind of encounters that form our children's hearts, minds, and souls occur as they come in contact with great books and learn to ask hard questions—and their minds are trained to think logically and well.

Sometimes that looks like a Latin declension, a math test, or an essay. Sometimes it looks like an afternoon spent reading poetry out loud, sipping cocoa, and watching the snow fall outside. We can't see what happens in the heart of our child when he meets Oliver Twist for the very first time or when he finds a dangling modifier and immediately knows that it is out of place (and why).

We get so distracted by pacing. *We've got to get through three more math lessons by Christmas*, we say to ourselves, *or else we'll get behind!* It is wise to evaluate our pace in light of our child—the trouble arises when we value the timeline over the child God gave us to teach.

Whether or not you finish your curriculum by May, get through all the lessons in the book, or do as much as you set out to do doesn't really matter, especially if you are merely "covering material" while diminishing your child's love for learning. Pacing doesn't matter if you are sacrificing mastery and love for truth, goodness, and beauty. Change the way you assess your success. The quality of study matters far more than the mere quantity of learning.

Lighten the Load

My husband enjoys backpacking in the wilderness. The first few times he went, he packed up his backpack like any other ordinary hiker and set out for his weekend with everything he thought he might want or need for his journey. He had made a list, gathered up supplies, and laid them upon the dining room table to make sure he had everything he needed before packing them into his backpack. Once loaded, the pack would easily weigh sixty pounds or more. He knew it would be heavy, but it was the beginning of the trail and enthusiasm was running high, so he'd hoist the pack onto his back and set out.

A mile in, that pack didn't feel like it was 60 pounds anymore—it felt like it was 200 pounds. The straps digging into his shoulders, he would slow to a creeping pace. Struggling to enjoy himself, he often wanted to quit. Sometimes he chucked nonessentials into the fire the night before packing back up to leave camp—after all, every ounce matters when the blisters on your feet are aching and your shoulders are sore.

These days, he doesn't do traditional backpacking. Now he does something called ultralight backpacking. The difference? Only what is absolutely essential goes into the pack. Every ounce is carefully considered, meticulously measured. No extra water (water can be filtered from sources along the trail) or snacks. Calculations are made beforehand so the hiker knows exactly what he will need. Many ultralight backpackers go so far as to cut their plastic toothbrushes in half. That small bit of plastic weighs almost nothing, but every ounce matters. Ounces add up to pounds, and pounds add to up to misery on the journey. If a hiker wants to enjoy the journey itself, get to his destination, and do more than sprawl flat on his back, panting for breath and feeling like he can't take another step, he simply can't bring any extra weight. Heb. 12:1

What implications does this have for homeschooling moms? Are you loading your backpack at the beginning of each new year with everything you think you may need or want for your journey? Or have you pared back? I assure you that by February—a mile into the trail—if your pack is weighed down by nonessentials, you'll feel as though you want to quit. The only way to combat that is to make sure that you aren't carrying too heavy a load in the first place.

Perhaps the biggest mistake homeschooling moms make as a whole is overcomplicating things. After all, curriculum is not something you buy. It is far too robust to be purchased online or checked off on a set of lesson plans. It is a set of encounters that form the soul and shape the intellect.

A stack of books. Hours of reading. Poetry. Long walks outside. Bike rides. Spelling words. Visits to the orchards. Sitting for hours with toddlers on laps, flipping through picture books, singing silly rhymes. Algebra problems. Library visits. Outings. Winter evenings spent huddled around a board game or listening to a story. Phonics. Handwork. A five-paragraph essay. Baking soda-and-vinegar volcanoes.

Mapwork. Drawing. Music. Conversations about everything under the sun. A garden. A grammar page. A memorized fact. A meal eaten with grandparents. A camping trip in August.

Live your life, relish ideas, wrestle. Remember, think, and converse. That is a curriculum you cannot buy, but your child's heart and mind will feast on it for years to come. It is full and robust, and yet at the very same time, it is simple. Its simplicity lies in knowing that we have chosen the better parts, the key ingredients that will have the greatest impact on our students' lives.

But how do we know what to choose? How do we simplify when there are so many good things to choose from, and the world seems wide and glorious and full of wonder and beauty? How do we ensure that our backpacks are not overloaded when we set out on the trail?

Clarifying Your Vision

Let's take some time to think practically about how we can teach our curriculum restfully and well.

For most of us this means considering how we can simplify and lighten our loads. We know that we must begin with surrender, that prayer is foundational, and that our daily grind is holy ground. But all of that sounds meaningless if we can't figure out how to implement rest into our actual, real, day-to-day plans.

In *The Screwtape Letters*, C.S. Lewis warns us against running around in a flood with fire extinguishers.[1]

Isn't that what we do? We notice a child is behind in a certain subject, that chores are not being done efficiently or well, that we aren't making progress like we want to be. Instead of assessing the real problem, we grab the closest fire extinguisher and start spraying the heck out of our kids. We're behind in math? More math! We're tired and overwhelmed? Revamp everything!

---

1. C.S. Lewis, *The Screwtape Letters* (San Francisco: HarperSanFrancisco, 2001), 138.

Many of us take on way too much. Education becomes a series of checkboxes and canned activities in our efforts to prove that learning is happening, even when it isn't. We feel turbulent when we try to facilitate this kind of frenzied, quantifiable learning. Often, we either become disconnected slave drivers or we give up altogether, accepting the illusion that happy, healthy relationships and rigorous home education simply cannot coexist.

There is another way. It boils down to stepping off the crazy train, rethinking the model within which we are operating, and intentionally setting out to participate in slow, sane education.

The first step in simplifying the curriculum is gaining clarity in our vision. If we don't know where we're going, what our purpose is for our children, our homeschool, and our family culture, it will be impossible to know what should go and what should stay. Even if we realize that something needs to be shaved off the syllabus in order to retain peace in the home, we don't know how to do the shaving. We've got to have clear vision in order to make the hard decisions of what to pare back.

I like to picture my children about twenty years down the road. I imagine they are enjoying a meal with friends and are asked about their growing-up years. "You were homeschooled," a friend says. Then she asks, "What was that like?" Which words, phrases, or sentences do I want my child to use when describing his or her homeschooled childhood?

Without contemplating too deeply on this, jot a few things down that are your own gut reactions to the question: What words do you want your children to use when they describe their homeschooled childhood? You don't really need to go that deep here—just skim the surface and you're bound to see what matters most to you.

There are a lot of things we can't control in parenting and homeschooling, but one thing we *can* do is shape the environment. For example, a couple of words/phrases/sentences that I want my children to use when describing their homeschooled childhood are *warm, conversational,* and *infused with truth, goodness, and beauty.*

I may not have control over the character qualities my children have as adults, or even whether or not they believe in the truths I have spent my life imparting to them. I *can* ensure that my home is one of warm conversations, filled with stories and beautiful experiences. I can do everything in my power to create an atmosphere that nourishes them in those ways so that even when I fail (and I will), and even when days are hard (as they will be), there is an underlying bedrock that will see us through the rough spots.

When I'm looking over my curriculum trying to decide what might need to go and what ought to stay, trying to shuck some nonessentials from my backpack, I can use those words I've chosen as a kind of litmus test. If I am trying to decide whether or not to keep a subject, a lesson, or a book, I run it through my filter. If something on the docket does not promote warmth, conversation, or the contemplation of the good, true, and beautiful, then it very well may need to go. Clarifying your vision with a few key words, phrases, or sentences is a practical way to begin with the end in mind and to focus on what really matters.

Five Ways to Simplify the Curriculum

A few principles are especially helpful to me in simplifying the curriculum I've either purchased or created for my children. I find it immensely helpful to tackle fewer subjects, integrate wherever possible, and really come to grips with the limitations of published resources. I also find it helpful to remind myself of the entire reason I'm homeschooling in the first place and then build in review time so that our time and energy is spent in the best possible way. Let's address each of those strategies.

1. Do Less

The most expedient way to simplify your curriculum is simply to track fewer subjects. Who says you need to do math, writing, literature, science, history, foreign language, religion, vocabulary, handwriting, art, music, and poetry all year long? Here's a little secret: You don't. And chances are, if you are trying to do all of those subjects, you very likely aren't doing a very good job at many of them.

Yes, we want a wide and generous education for our children. We want them to have a broad understanding of the big beautiful world, of the tragic failures and glorious breakthroughs in history, the lyrical beauty of prose and poetry, the order and art of mathematics. But as Dr. Christopher Perrin has taught me through the Latin maxim, *multum non multa (much not many)*, true breadth is achieved *through* depth. Our children get a broad education when they go deep into a few carefully selected subjects, not when they dabble in ten.

What most curricular models provide today is a survey of everything and mastery in nothing, so our children get an education that is a mile wide and an inch deep. That's not true education. We need to lead our children out of the shallows in order to dive in deep.

It's important that we select carefully when we take on this principle. If we are only going to focus on a few things, we'll want to make sure they are very good things, right? (Notice I didn't say "best." That's because the homeschooling mother's quest for the "best" is exasperating all on its own. That's not the way to teach from rest!)

If shaving entire subjects from your curriculum seems impossible or imprudent, consider simplifying *within* subjects. For example, in our home, we do geography the Charlotte Mason way.[2]

I give my older elementary-age child a blank outline map of a continent and an atlas, and ask her to label five countries and two bodies of water. She does that, and we put it away. Geography complete. The next day, I give her a brand-new blank outline map of the same continent and ask her to label what she remembers from yesterday. Sometimes she remembers it all, often she doesn't. That's OK. I give her the atlas once more and tell her to add the things she has forgotten, then to add three more countries and one more body of water. We put it away. The next day we follow the same procedure, and the next, and the next. This is an extremely simple and effective way to teach a child geography, and my children always learn quite a lot when we stick to this routine.

I have a tendency, however, to let other things creep in. I see a map skills workbook and add it to the curriculum, thinking that perhaps my child is missing something that is covered in the book. It only takes about fifteen or twenty minutes a week, after all, so there's no harm in adding it to our schedule, right? Then a friend at co-op tells me about the literature-based geography study she is doing with her children, and it sounds too wonderful to pass up, so I add that too. I find a computer game that drills children on their states and capitals, and a board game that helps them name countries by their shapes. Each of these seems simple enough and worthy, so slowly I add each to our docket until we are failing at all of them, ceasing to make meaningful progress and I feel like a failure at teaching geography.

This can happen in any subject, and it happens to many of us every single year (you'd think we'd learn!). Consider using the fourth strategy in this section, building in review times, to ensure that you haven't let extras crowd out the best parts of your curriculum.

---

2. Charlotte Mason was a nineteenth-century English educator and educational theorist who wrote about doing education that in many ways could be called "restful." One good book that introduces her educational thought and methods is Susan Schaeffer Macaulay's *For the Children's Sake: Foundations of Education for Home and School* (Wheaton, IL: Crossway, 2009).

Part Two: Curriculum Is Not Something You Buy

Another strategy for choosing which published resources to keep and which to remove is to ask yourself this: *If I did not already have this resource on my shelf, how much trouble would I go through to obtain it?* If the answer is "not much," it can likely be left off the plan.

2. Integrate

Realize that when you are reading aloud from *The Merry Adventures of Robin Hood*, you are not just doing literature. If you read it slowly, enjoying it, taking time to contemplate the ideas and discuss them with your kids, you are taking on history, geography, writing, vocabulary, theology, and philosophy as well. This isn't dabbling; it's wrestling.

I think of integration as a kind of curricular power punch. I want to choose published resources and subjects that are going to give me a lot of bang for my buck, so I try to think carefully before I add anything to our docket. How much value will this book/curriculum/assignment add? Is it going to add enough value to be worth the time it will take to engage with?

This is why in our family we choose to study Latin, prioritize reading aloud over almost everything else, and why I'm not a fan of time-consuming "hands-on" projects that eat up entire afternoons without allowing for mastery of material or engagement with big ideas. The nitty-gritty of this is going to look a little different for everybody, but the principle remains: Our lives are, by nature, integrated. Our school day should reflect that.

3. Understand the Limitations of Published Resources

Those printed resources you use (that you used to call curriculum, such as the math text or the handwriting workbook) are there to help you teach your students. Remember that the published resources are to be wielded by you, not to rule over you.

Whether or not you purchase an open-and-go curriculum doesn't really matter. You can pretty much forget all the heated discussions about whether you are caving in to school-at-home if you use traditional workbooks or a straight-from-the-box curriculum. I know successful homeschooling families who use textbooks and successful homeschooling families who eschew them. I don't think that's a relevant debate to be having if we want to teach from rest and become happy, content, peaceful, and effective homeschooling moms.

You are teaching your living, breathing, made-in-the-image-of-God students. The resources are there to help you do that. It's that simple—we just forget when we get all wrapped up in "getting through" all the math lessons before the end of May, or finishing every science experiment in the book before we call it good and move on. Remember, how far we progress in a book does not matter nearly as much as what happens in the mind and heart of our student, and for that matter, in ourselves. In fact, if a student grows to truly love an art (such as math), he is more likely to continue his study of math (or history, language, or literature) . . . in his free time.

You know this. I know this. But we've got to start living it. We are spinning our wheels because we're frantically trying to "get through" published curriculum as if turning the last page in the book by the beginning of summer vacation will somehow mean that our children learned something. The truth is, they do learn something from that. But it's not at all the message we want them to internalize.

We are teaching people, not books. In fact, a good book is often the best teacher—but we would do well to understand the limitations of curriculum. We need to stop trying to make it something that it's not, expecting it to yield what it was never intended to deliver.

4. Bake in Review Time

Do you have time set aside to consider and assess your homeschool? One practice that has helped me teach from rest is "baking in" review times—that is, planning ahead for times of assessment as the year progresses. I plan to reassess our schedule, our curriculum, and each student each term, which is every six weeks in our homeschool. Doing so helps me progress through daily, consistent work without falling prey to frenzy, anxiety, or an impulsive change in the curriculum.

I used to have a bad habit of changing published resources midstream. We'd reach a few rough spots in math and I'd immediately wonder if we needed to change to a different book. Perhaps we were using the wrong curriculum. Perhaps my student would be better served by something else. A homeschooling mother's mind plagued by such thoughts simply cannot be at peace. Even if I had spent a considerable amount of time choosing my curriculum before the year began, I would doubt my choices and worry. I tend toward impulsivity as well, so I would often follow up that anxiety and worry with quick-fix purchases and curriculum changes mid-year. This proved to be distressing for me and frustrating for my children.

The truth is, sometimes the curriculum *does* need a change. Sometimes a course or path is not meeting the needs of our students and we do need to come up with an alternative—but that is better considered calmly in a time set aside for such thinking, rather than in the throes of a stressful Tuesday morning while the dishwasher bubbles over and the toddler is throwing a fit.

Planning ahead for times of reassessment has freed me up to follow my plan of action. I no longer change the plan midstream. I plan six weeks at a time, and we follow that plan for six weeks, even if things aren't going as smoothly as I'd like.

After a six-week term, we have a week off. During that time, I consider each of my children and each part of their curriculum. Is it a good fit? Is it meeting their needs? Challenging them? Stretching them? Helping them to perceive truth, to remember, to think, and to speak? Perhaps we aren't making as much progress as we'd like to in math. Then it might be a good time to discuss with my husband the possibility of hiring a math tutor. Or maybe at the end of a term I realize that we didn't get to nearly as much history as I had hoped. As a result, I'll place history in a priority spot on the schedule for the next term.

Baking in a regular review time frees a homeschooling mom from making big decisions on the fly, while giving her the assurance that a time of assessment is coming—that if something isn't working, it can be remedied soon.

I have found this to be an invaluable part of teaching from rest.

5. Remember the Point

Once we allow ourselves to embrace the idea that curriculum is not something we buy, then we can really embrace the true goal of education: to order a child's affections and teach him to love that which is lovely. The point, then, is to put true, good, and beautiful ideas in front of our children and then to let them feast on them. To sit alongside them and model how one might go about dipping into the feast. We share a giant meal of ideas—contemplating, beholding, loving. We allow ourselves to be transformed by what we come in contact with.

> Finally, brethren, whatever is true, whatever is honorable, whatever is just, whatever is pure, whatever is lovely, whatever is gracious, if there is any excellence, if there is anything worthy of praise, think about these things. What you have learned and received and heard and seen in me, do; and the God of peace will be with you. (Philippians 4:8–9)

Take a good hard look at that subject or published resource before you add it to your lesson plan. Does it pass the Philippians 4:8 litmus test? Will it help you in your work of cultivating your child's affections for the true, good, and beautiful? If it does, then the peace of God will be with you and with your children. A child who loves and hates what he ought is a truly educated child—and that is the larger "point" of education.

I am in the habit of asking homeschooling mothers who are nearing or have reached the finish line what they did best. What would they change if they could go back in time? The perspective they offer is invaluable to me as a young mother. If I could, I would race ahead to myself twenty years from now and ask what I wish I had done differently. I can't do that, so instead I ask other women I trust and admire.

Time and time again, this is what these experienced moms tell me: Focus on the first things. Don't get wrapped up in the extraneous fluff. They never say, "Make sure your fourth grader is reading at the fourth grade level in the fourth grade." They don't tell me to worry over what the neighbors or my mother-in-law or anyone else thinks. They don't give me lists of their best curriculum choices and tell me to replicate them. They tell me to focus on relationships, to help my children preserve wonder and perceive truth, and to do each day's work as diligently as I can.

In his influential book *Beauty in the Word*, Stratford Caldecott wrote that the fundamental skills of humanity itself are remembering, thinking, and speaking.[3] That's really all there is to it. When I look at a potential curricular program or book to add to the plan for my child's year, I need to ask myself: *Will this help her remember? Will it help her think? Will it teach her to speak?*

3. Stratford Caldecott, *Beauty in the Word: Rethinking the Foundations of Education* (Tacoma, WA: Angelico Press, 2012).

Doing so helps me remember with utter clarity that we don't need to compartmentalize our schooling into artificial subjects. We need to encounter truth, goodness, and beauty at every turn. We need to come face to face with good ideas—with order, with logic, and with truth. We need to focus on the first things so that we may look back and know that we have done what we were called to do.

A Few Tips for Living This Out

- Keep it simple. Don't fall for gimmicky curricula that complicates what should be common sense.

- Read to your children every day (yes, even the older ones!). If you need some inspiration to make this a priority in your home, head to readaloudrevival.com. Set time aside for them to read on their own as well.

- Have your children write every day. It doesn't need to be book reports or historical essays. It can be a letter, an e-mail, a grocery list, or a journal entry. Make writing itself a priority.

- Do some math every day. Don't belabor it—do it every day and the consistency will do its work without long, drawn-out, arduous lessons.

Then, live your life. Do it in front of and with your kids. Plant a garden, keep house, learn to knit, cook, listen to audio books, visit new places, take factory tours, go to parks, sing, watch a play, go to museums, make music, take walks, care for pets, build things, watch films, listen to the stories of grandparents and elderly neighbors, go to church, celebrate the seasons, decorate the house for the holidays, create family traditions, play with art, visit the library and learn how to use it, go to the farmer's market, pick berries, read poetry and commit some to memory. Remember that children will learn well what they see in us, what they will inevitably imitate.

Perhaps most importantly, *put relationships above everything else.* God made a true, beautiful, and good world to relish. Don't get so distracted by thirty-six weeks of carefully plotted lesson plans that you miss the glory that is already yours for the taking.

How to Simplify the Schedule

Simplifying the curriculum is only half the battle—if our schedule is out of hand, we're still going to feel frenzied and hurried as we approach our learning. It doesn't really matter if we have the most beautiful, carefully thought-out plan if there aren't enough hours in the day to get to it.

If God expected you to get thirty-six hours' worth of work done in a day, He would have given you thirty-six hours to do it. If you have more to do than time to do it in, the simple fact is this: Some of what you are doing isn't on His agenda for you.

So how do we simplify the schedule? We must treat time as the finite resource it is, insist on margin, consider alternative scheduling options, and ultimately, remember that time isn't ours to begin with.

1. Start with a Time Budget

When you create your family budget, do you begin by listing all the things you'd like to be able to afford? Do you create a master list: a nice mortgage, a new SUV, a family vacation somewhere tropical, a food allowance that allows for eating out every single week? No? Then why on earth do you do it with your time?

Don't *begin* planning your day by listing all the things you want to pack in. Begin by looking at what God gave you (I'll give you a hint: twenty-four hours, and not all of them are for work).

The biggest problem I have with planning to use published curriculum resources is that they are all written for an entire school year, as if we need to do every subject all year long. That grates on me, because I'm quite sure it's why so many of us think we need to do every subject, every day, all year long. No wonder we struggle to teach from rest.

Take a hard look at the 168 hours in your week. Now consider your nonnegotiables: sleep, eat, shower, pray. Plug in meal preparation, rest and church on Sunday, and enough wind-down time at the end of each day to ensure a good night's sleep.

See what's left? You don't get any more than that, sister.

You have to begin with what you have, and what you have is a fixed amount of time. Doing it any other way is going to be an exercise in both frustration and anxiety, because we always want to do more than we have time to do. You can't base your family budget on your desire to spend Christmas in the Bahamas, and you can't base your homeschool schedule on your desire to do hands-on history, grow an organic vegetable garden, take weekly field trips, and study a new composer and artist every week of the year. We have to consider reality, and usually it's helpful to start there.

2. Insist on Margin

Once you figure out how much time you have in your daily budget of hours, fill only 80 percent of it.

Fact: If you plan three hours of schoolwork into three hours of work time, you will never get it done. You'll be chasing that list of to-dos and you'll never ever catch it. In his book *Margin: Restoring Emotional, Physical, Financial, and Time Reserves to Overloaded Lives*, Richard Swenson tells us, "Margin is the space between our load and our limits. It is the amount allowed beyond that which is needed. It is something held in reserve for contingencies or unanticipated situations. Margin is the gap between rest and exhaustion, the space between breathing freely and suffocating."[4]

If anyone can be sure that "unanticipated situations" will arise, it is a homeschooling mother. It's helpful to allow room for them, even if we can't necessarily see them coming.

If you want to be a peaceful homeschooling mother, and you want interested, engaged students, you have to schedule margin into your day. This is where it gets tricky, of course, because if you're going to

---

4. Richard Swenson, *Margin: Restoring Emotional, Physical, Financial, and Time Reserves to Overloaded Lives* (Colorado Springs, CO: NavPress, 1992), 81.

fill up only 80 percent of your day, you're going to have to seriously simplify your curriculum. There's no way around it.

Here's an example of a day with margin scheduled in, though there are an infinite number of ways to schedule your day. How you divide up and schedule work in your home will depend on a variety of factors, including your husband's work schedule, the number of babies or toddlers underfoot, and a whole host of other variables.

SAMPLE DAY WITH MARGIN		TIME ALLOTED	TIME SCHEDULED
8:00-10:00	Math (60 min.) Latin (30 min.) Phonics with younger kids (15 min.)	120 min.	105 min.
10:00-10:30	Break! Recess; play outside!		
10:30-12:00	Morning Time/Symposium (60 min.)	90 min.	60 min.
12:00-2:00	Lunch Quiet reading hour (60 min.) Play outside		
2:00-3:00	Writing (45 min.)	60 min.	45 min.
3:00-4:00	Independent work (45 min.)—spelling, typing, workbooks, etc.	60 min.	45 min.
	TOTAL	5.5 hours	4.25 hours

The key to the diagram above is to notice that 4.25 hours of schoolwork has been scheduled into 5.5 hours of the day. There is room, then, to breathe, to take what comes and see all of the unanticipated interruptions as pieces that make up a full and varied life. Life is made up of inconsistencies, so make sure your schedule provides guide rails for your day rather than serving as a measure of guilt or frustration as you do your best to keep things running smoothly.

3. Break Out of the Mold

God did not give you nine months a year in which to educate your children—He gave you twelve. Break free of the hold the public education system has on the way you think about your calendar, and you may just find you have a lot more time to work with than you thought you did.

In her e-book *Plan Your Year*, Pam Barnhill says, "While most states require a set number of days for school, not a single state requires you to school on any specific day. Not having to follow the traditional school calendar gives a family an amazing amount of freedom."[5]

One way to rearrange the schedule is to take advantage of the creative freedom you have regarding your calendar. For example, a year-round school schedule with frequent breaks may be a wonderful fit for your family dynamic. I know many homeschoolers who teach for six weeks, followed by a full week off. This breaks the school year into manageable terms, and lets both teachers and students commit to their work for a time without ever going so long that they get completely burned out.

Another option is to consider looping subjects. I do this in my home as an antidote to steamrolling over everyone in order to check off everything on my list. My problem with schedules, routines, and general task management systems is that most of them feed into my tendency to prioritize getting stuff done over building relationships. It's the nature of a list of tasks to put priority on the doing, and my ambitious personality takes that up a notch.

The concept of looping is simply this: Instead of assigning tasks to certain days of the week, list tasks and then tackle them in order, regardless of what day it is.

---

5. Pam Barnhill, *Plan Your Year: Homeschool Planning with Purpose and Peace* (Amazon Digital Services, 2014), 27.

For example, my morning read-aloud loop might look like this:

- *The Father Brown Reader: Stories from Chesterton* by Nancy Carpentier Brown
- *Story of the World* by Susan Wise Bauer
- *The Burgess Book of Birds* by Thornton Burgess
- *Read-Aloud Book of Bible Stories* by Amy Steedman

I have not assigned any of these books or subjects (literature, history, science, religion) to certain days. Every morning during the time I've allotted to reading aloud, we read a chapter from the next book on the list. In this way, if we miss our read-aloud time three Mondays in a row due to sick babies or teething toddlers, we are still on track.

Looping can be used wherever there is work that needs to be done regularly. Take anything you would otherwise be inclined to schedule into certain days of the week (Monday: literature, Tuesday: history, Wednesday: science . . . etc.) and put them on a loop instead. Now instead of feeling behind when the baby gets sick or you are running around putting out life's fires, you still make progress across the curriculum. You are never behind—you are right where you are supposed to be.

Using a loop schedule means we make progress on all of our planned subjects, no matter how many days we've had to forgo school in favor of real-life interruptions. During a particularly busy time, we may get through the loop only once over two weeks. When things are running well, we might get through the entire loop in a single week. The key is that the loop (and our curriculum!) serves us, not the other way around.

The loop is for tasks you don't need to do every day, but you want to tackle with some regularity. These tend to be content-based subjects such as history and science, not skill-based subjects such as Latin or math. Alternatively, you can loop within a daily task to offer some variation. For example, prayer needs to happen daily, but one could

Part Two: Curriculum Is Not Something You Buy

loop spiritual reading, *lectio divina*, personal devotions, and communal prayer to offer some variation within that daily prayer time.

I find that short loop schedules are more effective than long loop schedules. Having three to five items on a loop means we'll get to each task more often, which helps us progress through books and materials at a satisfactory rate. It also forces us to prioritize and think carefully before adding to our loop carelessly. Keep in mind that loop schedules can be rotated or changed up each term to keep the content fresh and engaging.

The following are some examples of loop schedules I have used in my home:

SAMPLE LOOP SCHEDULE FOR MORNING TIME

Literature and memory work happen daily, then loop through the following:

Poetry
Picture/Artist Study
Shakespeare
Composer Study
Literature Discussion

SAMPLE LOOP SCHEDULE FOR LANGUAGE ARTS

Grammar
Writing
Spelling/Dictation
Writing

SAMPLE LOOP SCHEDULE FOR
INDEPENDENT WORK
Nine-Year-Old
Keyboarding
Explode the Code
Keyboarding
Mapwork

SAMPLE LOOP SCHEDULE FOR
INDEPENDENT WORK
Eleven-Year-Old
Keyboarding
D'Aulaire's Greek Myths Study (Memoria)
Keyboarding
Mapwork

SAMPLE LOOP SCHEDULE FOR
INDEPENDENT WORK
Thirteen-Year-Old
Keyboarding
Logic
Keyboarding
Mapwork

Keep in mind that these activities are not tied to days of the week. Therefore, my nine-year-old may work through that entire loop twice each week because his loop activities only take about ten minutes. My thirteen-year-old, however, may only work through her loop once each week. That's the beauty of the loop. Everything gets approached in its own time on a regular schedule, regardless of what else is happening in life at the time.

4. Begin a Habit of Morning Time

Is there something you want to get to in your homeschool that constantly gets shuffled out of the day? Something like art appreciation, nature study, music, poetry, Shakespeare? Unfortunately, the good, true, and beautiful tend to take a backseat when we get deep into our homeschool year.

In my home, I find something even worse. By the time everyone has completed the basics for the day (you know—math, reading, writing . . . that kind of thing), we're all tired and ready for a change of pace, the house needs some attention, and it's late enough in the day that we need to move on to one of the many other parts of life.

Passing on the faith to my kids—arguably the entire reason I educate my children at home in the first place—gets squeezed out of the schedule. Those experiences that shape my children's souls and order their affections get set aside.

What to do? Two words: Morning Time.

In our home, this rarely happens in the morning, so we actually call it Symposium. "Symposium" has Greek roots and means "a convivial meeting . . . for drinking and intellectual conversation" or "a philosophical dialogue . . . dealing with ideal love and the vision of absolute beauty."[6]

This is a great excuse for pairing our learning with hot chocolate. I've also heard it called Deep Dive Monday or other such names, scheduled once per week, perhaps, or on a rotating basis.

It's simply a daily meeting incorporating subjects that are very important, but which often get shuffled out of the schedule for logistical reasons. Based firmly on the idea that the purpose of education is to teach our children to love that which is lovely, Morning Time/Symposium is time set aside for contemplation and discussion that offers an opportu-

---

6. *Dictionary.com*, s.v. "symposium," accessed May 28, 2015, http://dictionary.reference.com/browse/symposium?s=t.

nity for the homeschooling mom to connect her children directly with beauty, art, poetry, and the ideas that feed and nourish the soul.

Cindy Rollins first taught me about this concept. She described it in her blog *Morning Time Moms* as the "daily collection of little grains of time that add up to a lifetime of learning," the daily sowing of the seeds for the long haul.

"Morning Time is not about reaping a quick harvest of spinach or lettuce after a few cool weeks," she said. "[It's] about faithfully tending an orchard over long, long years knowing that the future harvest will be far more valuable than any quick crop. Maybe it isn't even an orchard—this is homeschool carbon which will produce a harvest of diamonds for those who have the patience and the courage to go for the long prize."[7]

What I find so helpful about Morning Time is that it places first things first—it's a liturgy of love. When you are trying to teach from a state of rest, employing a Morning Time routine helps you place the emphasis on loving, going deep, and relishing rather than on "getting through." Nothing stirs up a mom's anxiety more than pressure to "get through."

How It Works

Choose the time you will do Morning Time each day. It can be twenty minutes or two hours, though if you are just starting out, build up slowly so you don't get overwhelmed and your children don't revolt.

Now, during that time, encounter beauty with your children. Read Scripture, recite poetry, read from a classic. Look at a piece of great art and talk about it, then choose another book and read that. Drill your catechism. Discuss what you read together. Diagram a sentence together as a family. Morning Time is when you gather for subjects that the whole family can do together. The key is that it happens regularly and takes priority over everything else.

7. Cindy Rollins, "What Is Morning Time and Why Bother?" *Morning Time Moms* (blog), August 5, 2014, http://www.ordo-amoris.com/2014/08/what-is-morning-time-and-why-bother.html.

Small increments of time add up to years, but that can be so hard to remember when you're in the thick of it. Cultivating a habit of encountering truth, beauty, and goodness will not be time wasted. It will simplify your schedule and your curriculum, and will go a long way to calm any unrest you may feel about all the things you don't usually get around to doing.

"Over the years Morning Time became the structure on which I built our school," Cindy once wrote. "I started our version of this by using the time to cover the things that I loved and the things I did not want the children to miss out on in the everyday stress of schooling. I was basically following my heart. Only later did I come to realize that the successes of our homeschool were almost entirely rooted in Morning Time."[8]

Babies and Toddlers in the Morning-Time Mix:

Babies and toddlers present a unique challenge at Morning Time, and I am no stranger to those hurdles! Here are a few simple tips for keeping on when the smallest in the family threaten to thwart the whole affair.

Spend Time with the Smallest Children before You Begin: I find that if I can spend a little one-on-one time playing with, reading to, or otherwise doting on my smallest children first, then they are less clingy

---

8. Cindy Rollins, *Morning Time Moms* (blog—), article no longer available.

for the rest of the day. Fill up their tank with mom's love and attention before you sit down to focus on your older kids.

Create a Morning-Time Box: The Morning-Time box only comes out at this time of day. Rotate what is in the box every now and again to keep it interesting. Allow your small children to play with whatever is in the box at the kitchen table or on a blanket on the floor. Some ideas for what to put inside:

- playdough
- Color Wonder markers and paper (no mess!)
- a rice or bean sensory tub
- a tub of water with funnels, measuring spoons and cups, etc.
- animal figurines (my kids love the Toobs from Safari Limited)
- a snack in a muffin tin (they can move their snack from liner to liner, taking bites here and there but mostly playing!)
- paintbrush and a small dish of water (to be used in the high chair; this also makes a fabulous outdoor activity with fat brushes and a bucket of water—tell your small child to "paint the deck" while you read aloud to the others on a picnic blanket)
- pattern blocks
- chunky wooden puzzles
- lacing cards

Have realistic expectations. You just aren't going to be able to have long, luxurious Morning Time sessions while there are toddlers underfoot! Use the principles we've talked about in this book to help you choose the most important things to tackle during Morning Time, and focus on those. Remember that there are many years that make up a childhood. You can get to other beautiful subjects you long to teach another year.

5. Remember Whose Time You're On (Hint: It Isn't Yours)

Finally, the best way to shed frustration and angst about the schedule is simply to remember that your time isn't yours to begin with—it's His. We may be bound by the constraints of the clock, but the God of the Universe is not. Giving Him our days and our minutes will yield more fruit than we could ever hope to yield on our own.

When we're working to simplify our schedules, the temptation to multitask can become overwhelming. It's true that becoming a habitual multitasker will mean that you check a lot more off your list at the end of the day. It also invariably means that you will have missed the critical point of truly educating your child. She is not a project to be managed but a soul to be cultivated. Let's consider why we ought to do the right thing at the right time and focus on one main task at a time.

The Right Thing at the Right Time

When you are reading a picture book to your small child, preparing dinner, or helping your child draw a map or tackle a math problem, are you *also* doing something else? The problem with multitasking does not lie in doing more than one thing at a time. The problem arises when you miss a "now moment" because you are wrapped up in some imaginary one that hasn't happened yet (or won't happen at all).

If you are like me, you may be helping your child add a picture to his history timeline, but you are also brewing what is coming next. You're thinking about what you'll add to the timeline next, which books might help you flesh out your history lesson, where you can go to get a good period map. You're making your grocery list in your head while you read *The Story about Ping* for the millionth time. You're boiling the pasta, checking e-mail, and breaking up a sibling squabble, all at once. In the meantime, you may have gotten through the lesson, turned the last page of the picture book, fed your clan, cleaned out your e-mail in-box, fixed (albeit temporarily) the discord between the kids, but you didn't relish or truly attend to any of it.

I want to squeeze everything possible out of every minute of my day—it's probably a personality thing. If I know the soup won't be ready for ten minutes, I try to fit in a reading lesson with one child while telling another to set the table. Oh, and perhaps I could nurse the twins while I'm at it. That would be ten minutes well spent! Dinner ready, table set, reading lesson done, babies fed!

But there is no prize for the mom who checks the most boxes on her to-do list. (Darn it anyway, I would win!) There just isn't a way to steep yourself fully in this moment if you multitask your way through it. With the exception of automatic behaviors such as walking and talking, our brains can only attend to  one thing at a time. What we usually think of as multitasking is actually task switching, and it is both an inefficient and ineffective way to work.

By definition, to be efficient is to achieve maximum productivity with minimum wasted effort or expense. But relationships don't flourish or grow that way. Relationships need time, spent lavishly. Homeschooling is all about relationships, and relationships just aren't efficient.

This can be a real struggle for those of us who homeschool. We have so much to get to: the laundry, meal planning and preparation, housework, errands, running children hither and yon, making time and space

Part Two: Curriculum Is Not Something You Buy

for other daily efforts such as exercise, our spouses, and our personal development. We want to be good stewards of our time, but maybe that time is best spent "carelessly" when it comes to people.

We've all heard of folks at the end of their lives, looking back and wishing they had spent more time with the people they loved. I'm not sure I've ever heard someone wish they had spent more time getting things done.

How about at the end of the day? When you sneak into your child's bedroom to drop one more kiss on her cheek as she sleeps, will you wish you had gotten to a few more loads of laundry? Decluttered one more closet? Run just a few more errands? Or will you wish you had stopped to stare into her eyes, to pull her onto your lap and talk about something she's thinking about? Will you wish you had wasted a perfectly good five minutes listening to her ramble on about what she found under a rock while she was playing outside?

These things take time. They cannot be done efficiently.

What if, instead of trying to make the most of our time, we worked harder at savoring it? What if we were more intentional and lavish with our time and more detached from our checklists? Getting caught up in plans for what is coming next or trying to squeeze everything possible into this moment right now is a surefire way to miss the gift of this moment, today, and it is a certain path to anxiety. Teaching from rest doesn't mean we aren't planning ahead (in fact, we will likely need to use written plans and checklists), and it definitely doesn't mean we are lazy. It means that we are doing one thing at a time, and we do that thing with all our heart.

I wonder what Jesus's ministry would have looked like if He was as obsessed as we are with "making the most of our time." As Kevin DeYoung said in *Crazy Busy: A (Mercifully) Short Book about a (Really) Big Problem*:

> *Jesus did not do it all.* Jesus didn't meet every need. He left people waiting in line to be healed. He left one town to

preach to another. He hid away to pray. He got tired. He never interacted with the vast majority of people on the planet. He spent thirty years in training and only three years in ministry. He did not try to do it all. And yet, he did everything God asked him to do.[9]

So how do we break the habits of productivity and efficiency that we have been mothering and teaching with for years, perhaps decades? "Keep cutting back until there is peace in your home," says Nancy Kelly, a Charlotte Mason Consultant and blogger at Sage Parnassus.[10] If education is in part an atmosphere, then creating an atmosphere of peace should be of utmost importance.

Part of our problem with cutting back is that we lack clarity in our vision. We aren't clear enough on our goals or on how to use our day to support those goals, so we think whatever we are doing right now is either not what we are supposed to be doing, or that it simply isn't enough.

Well, *are* we doing what we are supposed to be doing? Have we thought through the schedule ahead of time and simplified so that we know the most important thing we should be doing at two thirty on a Thursday afternoon?

The whole underlying principle is that we have to decide ahead of time what the most important thing is to do at any given time in order to banish the worry that we might not actually be doing the best thing possible in this moment. Flying by the seat of our pants or "living in the moment" without taking the time to carefully assess what we *ought* to be doing at any given moment is a recipe for failure. Remember, we want to love what we ought to love, and shun what we ought to shun. When you think you have a general plan for your day, pray over it. Ask God to reveal to you where you are missing the point.

9. Kevin DeYoung, *Crazy Busy: A (Mercifully) Short Book about a (Really) Big Problem* (Wheaton, IL: Crossway, 2013), 50.
10. Brandy Vencel, "Secrets from Charlotte Mason on Scheduling for Peace," *AfterThoughts* (blog), accessed June 11, 2015, available at: http://afterthoughtsblog.net/2014/06/secrets-from-charlotte-mason-on.html.

Once we are sure we're doing what we should be, we have to ask ourselves, *Is it enough?* If you are reading a picture book to a toddler or working through a spelling lesson with your nine-year-old, is it enough to spend this chunk of time on that one small thing? If you spend the entire time you had set aside for math working through one single math problem, helping your child iron out her misunderstandings and really get a good handle on the concept at hand, can you close the math book for the day and feel successful? Or will you let that whole page of math problems taunt you?

> Little drops of water,
> Little grains of sand,
> Make the mighty ocean
> And the pleasant land.
>
> So the little moments,
> Humble though they be,
> Make the mighty ages
> Of Eternity.
> . . . .
>
> Little deeds of kindness,
> Little words of love,
> Help to make earth happy
> Like the Heaven above.[11]

It may be just a little drop of water, but if you can manage to take the long view, you will see that these little moments, done faithfully, add up to quite a lot more than just a puddle. Done faithfully and mindfully, day in and day out over years, they "make the mighty ocean."

Yes. That one thing you are doing is enough.

Today, as you go about your teaching and mothering, periodically stop. Ask yourself, "What am I doing right now?" If the answer is

---

11. Julia Abigail Fletcher Carney, "Little Things," in *Famous Poems from Bygone Days*, ed. Martin Gardner (Mineola, NY: Dover Publications, 1995), 36.

"helping my child diagram a sentence," then diagram the sentence. Do it without making a to-do list in your head or fretting about all the other subjects you still have to get to that day. If the answer is "cooking dinner," then do it with everything you have. Don't run off to check your e-mail while the sauce is simmering. Let it simmer. Talk to your kids. Turn on some quiet music and just relax into the moment.

Today, do less. Do it well.

Part Three:
Be Who You Are!

First keep the peace within yourself,
   then you can also bring peace to others.

—Thomas à Kempis, *The Imitation of Christ*

The Truth about You

Several years ago I was told by a lady that she could never home-school because she wasn't a salt-dough-map-making kind of mom. I get that. Nothing makes me groan like reading, in a set of lesson plans, complex instructions telling me how to mummify a chicken or create a raised-relief depiction of Egypt. Truth be told, I'm not all that convinced that homeschooling mothers need to engage in such elaborate activities to make learning worthwhile.

A few years into homeschooling, one thing is abundantly clear to me: A peaceful and happy mother is the real key to successful homeschooling. Choosing excellent materials is important, of course. Establishing a healthy daily routine is enormously helpful. Developing an active social life is essential. We can read up on every curriculum on the market, listen to podcasts, devour articles, attend conferences, participate in co-ops or support groups, but none of this will have the same impact on the life of a homeschooling family as a peaceful and happy mother.

To become peaceful and happy, you've got to figure out what's true about you. What creates an environment in which you can thrive? How can you work with your own innate strengths and weaknesses so that your homeschool will be happy and humming, even if you never construct a sugar cube pyramid or help your kids put together a single diorama?

Yes, there are oodles of blogs in which crafty moms showcase all the incredibly wonderful things they are doing with their kids. Good for them! I don't mean that sarcastically at all—I really do mean, good for them. What beauty to watch a mom thrive alongside her children.

But there is more than one way. If you aren't a crafty mom—if the thought of letting your child loose with a can of glitter and a bottle of glue makes you break out in hives (join the club!), then shut your Internet browser and quit looking at Pinterest long enough to figure out what would help *you* thrive.

I have spent a lot of time (too much, actually) thinking about my children's learning styles. I've pondered how to meet their unique needs and provide them with learning opportunities based on their own interests. It never occurred to me, during all that reading and pondering, that I just might burn out if I didn't consider my own personality and my own teaching style as well. If I'm not thriving as a homeschooling mother, my students are going to suffer for it.

We must look ourselves squarely in the eye and decide what is true about how we operate best, then base our homeschools on those truths, playing to our strengths and providing for our weaknesses. The result? The children benefit tremendously, regardless of their unique learning styles.

When I stop to consider what's true about me, a few things come immediately to mind:

- I love reading aloud. It is my favorite thing to do with the kids.

- I have the most energy in the morning, and very little by midafternoon.

- In general, I plan ahead and write everything down. Our calendar, our menu, our homemaking routine, what we need at the store, what I want to tell my friend when I call her . . . everything.

- I detest "pea and stick" work (making salt dough maps, building pyramids with sugar cubes, creating a diorama—that kind of thing).

- I also really don't care for worksheets. I'd much rather just talk to my child to find out what's happening inside his head.

- I enjoy teaching life skills. I'd rather teach my kids how to bake a cake than how to make a paper-bag puppet.

- I feel most productive when checking off lists. I am encouraged to continue when I can see quantifiable results.

- I need certain times of day blocked out for school time (or chore time, or prayer time) to ensure that such activities happen every day. Otherwise I am easily distracted and tend to lack necessary self-discipline.

- I am inspired by beauty. Making it beautiful (a checklist, a notebook, a space in my home) ensures that I will be much happier working with it.

- I have a tendency to start strong and then fizzle. This means I must have good habits in place to help carry me through when I'm feeling less enthusiastic.

You don't have to be a homeschooling superstar to feel good about the kind of educator you are for your kids. Just be yourself. Embrace who you are. You are made in the image and likeness of God, and you have exactly what you need to be the mother that He wants you to be.

Your own tendencies are likely different than mine. My own weakness is to start strong and then fizzle. You may struggle with starting at all—shooting from the hip and failing to plan in a way that meets the needs of your family and helps you make slow and steady progress in the areas that matter most. Or perhaps your weakness is acting as a drill sergeant, forgetting to make the curriculum work for you, and making yourself (and your children) the slave of the published resource.

Knowing the truth about you doesn't mean that "you are who you are" and that you aren't being called to stretch and grow appropriately. One of the pitfalls of taking an assessment of our vices and virtues is that we often lean on them as a crutch. If I know that my own tendency is to fly by the seat of my pants and fail to spend some time on the front end prayerfully and carefully setting a course for our year, I can either use that knowledge to improve upon my weaknesses and grow in virtue, or I can lean on it as an excuse to keep doing what I've been doing. There's a fine balance here between knowing about yourself so that you may grow in virtue and overcome sin, and knowing about yourself and leaning on those vices as excuses.

That said, figure out what drives you and then let your kids shine within the atmosphere you create. Trying to be something you're not, trying hard to provide your kids with the education that the homeschooler-next-door is giving hers, will burn you out and make you want to quit the whole project entirely. You've got to remember *who* you are and *Whose* you are.

I became a peaceful and happy homeschooling mom when I learned to be content with my own preferences and no longer strove to be like the women whose strengths are different from my own. I began working to overcome my weaknesses and growing in grace where I had been lacking. And then I learned that in the end, I'm just me. And that's just the kind of homeschooling mom I want to be.

Plan to Breathe

Do you bubble over with zeal, enthusiasm, and interest? Are you so delighted in something—anything—that you can't wait to share it with others? Our days don't have to throb with excitement, but when you think back on the teachers that impacted you most, I bet you remember one who wasn't burned out and distracted, just dragging you through a lesson plan in order to get through.

If you find yourself so tired that you can't feel excited about anything, then maybe you need to carve out time for a little cultivation of yourself. Shuck something else that is oh-so-important off the curriculum for a week and use that time slot to go for a walk every day instead. Bring a field guide. Pack a picnic. Or don't, if the thought of doing such a thing wears you out.

What you must do, however, is find a way to relish this ordinary Wednesday. Do whatever you need in order to behold the face of God in your children and to delight in them.

There is always more to do. There are always more subjects to cover, more lessons to get to. You can work to the point of exhaustion and still feel lacking. Or you can take this day, today, this gift of the present, and you can live it. You can seek first the Kingdom of God here on earth, and by doing so, model the best kind of living to your kids. Andrew Kern, founder and president of CiRCE Institute, states:

> The most important thing every teacher should under-
> stand is that teaching is the art of being imitated. If you
> want a student to perceive a truth, you have to embody
> it. That's what teaching is. When you teach, whether you
> intend to or not, you are saying to your students, "imitate
> me." Make yourself worthy of imitation.[12]

If we would like our children to practice deep thinking, contemplate big ideas, and relish truth and beauty as they go about their learning, perhaps we should make that a habit ourselves.

This is countercultural (as are so many worthwhile pursuits, don't you think?). We moderns are obsessed with productivity—it goes against the grain to stop checking things off a list long enough to really go deep, enjoy, and steep ourselves in a new idea or skill.

"When God rested after six days of creation, he was not tired," Dr. Christopher Perrin tells us in his online article "Learning and Leisure: Developing a School of *Scholé*":

---

12. Andrew Kern, "Forging a Likeness," *CiRCE Magazine*, November 2013: 6.

Part Three: Be Who You Are!

He celebrated and blessed his creation (Gen. 2:3). The Sabbath rest and the regular feasts were not given so that God's people would do nothing, though it did mean ceasing from typical daily labor. Rather it was meant as a time for a particular kind of robust activity—feasting, celebration and blessing. The Sabbath rest is not the mere cessation of labor, but the orientation of the human to his highest end—the "work" of leisure, the "work" of praising, serving, feasting and blessing.[13]

Do you have this kind of Sabbath in your own life? Making time for delight in our own lives is not about adding to the to-do list, but rather about kindling the flame and igniting enthusiasm. There are a million ways to encounter the truth, goodness, and beauty in the world every day. For some it may look like learning to watercolor, for others reading through a book of poems by T.S. Eliot. You might learn how to dip candles, identify the trees in your neighborhood, write blog posts, or take care of an aquarium tank full of fish.

Of course, we must remember: Rest is not the opposite of work, but rather work of a different order. Josef Pieper describes this for us in *Leisure: The Basis of Culture*:

> Leisure, it must be clearly understood, is a mental and spiritual attitude—it is not simply the result of external factors, it is not the inevitable result of spare time, a holiday, a weekend or a vacation. *It is, in the first place, an attitude of mind, a condition of the soul*, and as such utterly contrary to the ideal of "worker" in each and every one of the three aspects under which it was analyzed: work as activity, as toil, as social function. . . . For leisure is a receptive attitude of mind, a contemplative attitude, and *it is not only the occasion but also the capacity for steeping oneself in the whole of creation*.[14]

---

13. Christopher Perrin, "Learning and Leisure: Developing a School of *Scholé*," *Inside Classical Education* (blog), November 24, 2010, http://insideclassicaled.com/?p=295.
14. Josef Pieper, *Leisure: The Basis of Culture* (San Francisco: Ignatius Press, 2009), 46, emphasis added.

Restful learning is not throwing all care to the wind, eschewing worthy goals such as mastery of the math facts, the ability to read hard books, or cultivating the art of writing persuasively and well. Remember the account of creation—six days the Lord labored before He rested on the Sabbath. Rest, then, is not the absence of work or toil. It is the absence of anxiety or frenzy.

This won't look the same for all of us, but the one common thread is that to imitate delight in our lives is to mindfully engage in truth, goodness, and beauty as a regular part of life. If we long to cultivate *scholé* in our homes and in our children, then we must cultivate it in ourselves as well.

The Truth about Them

Tell me this: If you could have a guarantee that your child would be a National Merit Scholar and get into a prestigious college, have good work habits and a successful career, but that your relationship with him would be destroyed in the process, would you do it?

Why not? Because you are made to love, that's why. We care about our relationships more than about our accomplishments. That's the way God made us.

So why don't we live that way? Why, come a damp and gloomy day in March, do we yell over a math lesson or lose our temper over a writing assignment? Why do we see the lessons left to finish and get lost in an anxiety-ridden haze? We forget that we are dealing with a soul, a precious child bearing the image of God, and all we can see is that there are only a few months left to the school year and we are still only halfway through the math book.

C.S. Lewis tells us in *The Weight of Glory*:

It is a serious thing to live in a society of possible gods and goddesses to remember that the dullest, most uninteresting person you talk to may one day be a creature which, if you saw it now, you would be strongly tempted to worship, or else a horror and a corruption such as you now meet, if at all, only in a nightmare. All day long we are, in some degree, helping each other to one or the other of these destinations. It is in the light of these overwhelming possibilities, it is with the awe and the circumspection proper to them, that we should conduct all of our dealings with one another, all friendships, all loves, all play, all politics. There are no ordinary people. You have never talked to a mere mortal.[15]

These children, entrusted to our care, are not mere mortals.

When you are performing mommy triage—that is, when you have a crisis moment and have to figure out which fire to put out first—always choose your child. It's just a math lesson. It's only a writing assignment. It's a Latin declension. Nothing more.

But your child? He is God's. And the Almighty put him in your charge for relationship. Don't damage that relationship over something so trivial as an algebra problem. And when you do (because you will, and so will I), repent.

Education entails repentance, the constant turning back to our Creator and letting Him pick us up when we fall. Isaiah 30:15 says, "For thus said the Lord GOD, the Holy One of Israel, 'In returning and rest you shall be saved; in quietness and in trust shall be your strength.'" Repentance, then, goes hand in hand with rest.

We like to feed our egos. When our children perform well, we can puff up with satisfaction and pat ourselves on the back for a job well done. But as important as it is to give our children a solid education (and it is important, don't misunderstand me), it is far more important that we

---

15. C.S. Lewis, *The Weight of Glory* (New York: HarperOne, 2009), 45–46.

love them well. Our children need to know that the most important thing about them is not whether they finished their science curriculum or scored well on the SAT. Their worth is not bound up in a booklist or a test score.

Take a moment. Take ten. Look deep into your child's eyes. Listen, even when you're bored. Break out a game or an old picture book you haven't read in ages. Resting in God means relaxing into the knowledge that He has put these children in our care to nurture, and that looks different than charging through the checklist.

Your children are not ordinary kids or ordinary people, because there are no ordinary kids or ordinary people. They are little reflections of the Almighty.

What Happens to Ants after They Die?

One of the first memories I have of our early homeschooling days happened when my oldest kids were five and three. This was a new adventure for us, but I was feeling very prepared. Forty-seven how-to books into my homeschooling career, I had researched the methods, mastered the lingo, and formulated a plan. Butcher paper taped to the wall, Sharpie in hand, I was ready to fling open the doors on the whole wide world from our little kitchen table.

We were beginning a unit study on ants, and our class time began with a brainstorm: "What do we want to find out about ants?" I asked.

My then three-year-old scrunched up her face, deep in thought. Her little voice carried a reverent tone as she asked the first thing that popped into her head: "What happens to ants after they die?"

Silence. I had been anticipating the important questions. You know, "What do ants eat?" and "How many make up a colony?" I was not prepared for this. I was prepared to dive into a dissertation on the diet and lifestyle of an ant, and I was immediately rendered speechless.

I looked down at my color-coded poster of the ant's anatomy, my ant-related word list, my ant farm diagram. I realized with acute clarity that my curriculum had nothing on my three-year-old.

This small child, all bouncy curls and sticky peanut-butter-and-jam lips—she asked the profound question that surpassed "the curriculum."

Even now as an eleven-year-old, everything she does takes twice as long as I think it should and requires her full attention. If she is interrupted mid-sentence, she completely loses her train of thought. As a small child, she spent much of each day in silence, caring for her "Mmm"—the special blanket she pushed in the swing, read to at naptime, and tucked in at night. Careful—methodical even—in her random sort of way, as a toddler she often chastised me, "Don't go so fast. You're moving too fast for my insides." Today a large portion of her time is spent collecting bits of nature, painting rocks, sitting in her room, and just contemplating. It's just how she lives—quietly going about her day, taking care of the important things.

The important things. For her, it isn't at all critical what an ant eats. In fact, it doesn't really matter if the ant eats at all. Not unless its eternity is sorted out.

If only I could learn from her! My mind races before I climb out of bed each morning. I'm always doing four things at once, not really giving full attention to any one person or thing. If I'm pushing a child on the swing, I'm also opening a letter, on the phone with the pediatrician's office, and burning dinner. Even when it comes to putting my feet up, I get distracted by the sink full of dishes or the pile of mail. Some people call it multitasking, as though it's a skill to be desired and honed, but I know it's really a lack of focus—a refusal to seek out the important things. To read a book to my kids without making a grocery list and a weekend itinerary at the same time requires me to be fully present—to stop the spinning wheels racing in my head and pay attention.

When Jesus said, "Lord, You have hidden these things from the wise and learned, and revealed them to little children," this is exactly what He meant (see Matthew 11:25; Luke 10:21). In so many ways, I draw closer to God by observing my daughter's interactions with Him. Her eating, sleeping, and breathing is a testament to His presence—His desire for me to focus on what's important.

My Sharpie wobbled a little as I carefully wrote the question down on our large sheet of butcher paper: *What happens to ants after they die?*

I stop and wonder whether any other questions are really necessary. After all, even though as a wife and mother I wear many hats and shoulder endless responsibilities, the most important thing is not whether my kids can label the anatomy of an insect or describe the tunneling patterns of a harvester ant. It's what happens after death that really counts.

Walking on Water

> Then he made the disciples get into the boat and go before him to the other side, while he dismissed the crowds. And after he had dismissed the crowds, he went up on the mountain by himself to pray. When evening came, he was there alone, but the boat by this time was many furlongs distant from the land, beaten by the waves; for the wind was against them. And in the fourth watch of the night he came to them, walking on the sea. But when the disciples saw him walking on the sea, they were terrified, saying, "It is a ghost!" and they cried out for fear. But immediately he spoke to them, saying, "Take heart, it is I; have no fear."
>
> And Peter answered him, "Lord, if it is you, bid me come to you on the water." He said, "Come." So Peter got out of the boat and walked on the water and came to Jesus; but when he saw the wind, he was afraid, and beginning to sink he cried out, "Lord, save me." Jesus immediately reached out his hand and caught him, saying to him, "O man of little faith, why did you doubt?" And when they got into the boat, the wind ceased. And those in the boat worshiped him, saying, "Truly you are the Son of God." (Matthew 14:22–33)

You are Peter. You, mother of that little flock of children you have there. Motherhood is a mad and swirling sea. It is wind beating on waves, storm on the horizon, tumult on the waters. It's bigger than you can ever hope to be. You are clinging to your boat, quite a distance from land now, and the storm is rougher than you imagined it would be.

And then God calls you to homeschool—to step out on the water. *"Come."* Homeschool? Must I take this on too? *"Take heart; it is I. Have no fear."*

And so you do. You step out of the boat. Amazingly, the waves do not overtake you. You feel the wind beating hard, threatening to overwhelm you; you keep your eyes fixed on Jesus, hear the clarity of His voice as He bids you come. You do it. You are walking on water.

As happens to all homeschooling mothers, doubts creep in. Maybe your family thinks you are crazy, maybe your neighbors begin to whisper about you. You feel inadequate, and you wonder how you will possibly do this. Your children spend days on end fighting and bickering; you lose your temper; you get frustrated and angry and overwhelmed. You realize your middle schooler is behind on math, that you never taught your second grader how to tie his shoes or what his address is, and you watch as your house falls apart around you. Just like Peter, the wind is against you and you begin to sink.

Welcome to the water. It's kind of cold, isn't it? Yes, I know. I've been there. Might I suggest you read that passage in Matthew again? Go ahead. I'll wait.

Immediately. They cried out in fear, and He *immediately* spoke to them. Peter called, "Lord, save me," and He *immediately* reached out His hand.

Maybe your task seems impossible. In fact, it probably *is* impossible! So is walking on water, and Jesus didn't seem to strain much to help Peter do that. Even Peter! Sinful, prideful, impulsive Peter! The one who rejected the Lord at His time of need—the one whom the Lord called from a fisherman's small and insignificant life to fulfill a place in His kingdom that we can barely comprehend.

If we cry out, He will *immediately* reach out His hand.

Fix your eyes on Jesus. Don't you dare take your eyes off Him, because you will surely sink. And when you do, cry out. O you of little faith, why did you doubt? *He's got this.* He always did.

"And when they got into the boat, the wind ceased."

Let It Lie

Sometimes we just need to get out of the way. Our children were born curious, born with a thirst to know. It's their nature to want to learn.

In her book *A Philosophy of Education*, the great educator Charlotte Mason said that when we put children in direct contact with great ideas, "Teachers shall teach less and scholars shall learn more."[16]

Any homeschooling parent who has observed her own children for any length of time will know this to be true. Meaningful learning happens when our children wrestle directly with great ideas—not as a result of our repackaging those great ideas, but when they interact with the ideas themselves.

Our children are not projects. If, by the grace of God, we can manage to remember that our children are all made in His image—and more importantly, if we can treat them as such despite the mess and the chaos—then we will really be able to teach from rest. Therein lies the reason we've taken on this arduous task of home education at all—because a government school would not see our children as the image bearers that they are. After reciting the Pledge of Allegiance, there would be no Morning Offering, no Nicene Creed. They would miss countless opportunities to love on their siblings and form deep, meaningful encounters with each other, with us, and with material chosen specifically to nurture their souls. We want all else to pale in comparison to our quest toward honor, virtue, and wisdom.

Our days, though messy, loud, chaotic, and sometimes completely overwhelming, can be filled with great peace. We just have to get out of the way.

Please note: You do not need to have a "productive" homeschool day to please the Savior. You do not need to have a clean house to please the

---

16. Charlotte Mason, *A Philosophy of Education* (Wheaton, IL: Tyndale House, 1989), 8.

Savior. You do not even need to have well-behaved kids to please Him. Ultimately it doesn't matter if you hit every math problem, get through an entire spelling lesson, or whether your child loves learning the way you want him to. You are cultivating your child like a tree, and trees will bear fruit in time. We are taking the long view. Consistency over time goes a long way toward tending our orchard. Faithfully tending to your work each day *is* what success looks like for the homeschooling mother.

What matters is that we seek to imitate Christ. That we order our loves so that our hearts better reflect His. Many days, checklists will go untouched, books will go unread, and ducks will not line up in a row, no matter how much we strive.

Cease striving. St. Jerome once said, "It is our part to offer what we can, his to finish what we cannot."[17]

There is much to be learned in the muddle, and Chesterton tells us that anything worth doing is worth doing badly.[18]

We offer ourselves to God, we introduce our children to beauty and goodness and truth, and cease our anxious striving. That is the way to teach from rest.

17. St. Jerome, quoted in Danielle Bean and Elizabeth Foss, *Small Steps for Catholic Moms: Your Daily Call to Think, Pray, and Act* (Notre Dame, IN: Ave Maria Press, 2013), n.p.
18. Chesterton, *Orthodoxy*, 8. This is worth doing.

Scholé *in the Teacher's Life*

I wonder how many of us are trying to pour wine from empty pitchers. The account of the wedding at Cana from the second chapter of the Gospel of John strikes me whenever I read it, because even when He is performing His very first miracle, the Lord doesn't start with nothing: He starts with what the people have.

> On the third day there was a marriage at Cana in Galilee, and the mother of Jesus was there; Jesus also was invited to the marriage, with his disciples. When the wine failed, the mother of Jesus said to him, "They have no wine." And Jesus said to her, "O woman, what have you to do with me? My hour has not yet come." His mother said to the servants, "Do whatever he tells you."
>
> Now six stone jars were standing there, for the Jewish rites of purification, each holding twenty or thirty gallons. Jesus said to them, "Fill the jars with water." And they filled them up to the brim. He said to them, "Now draw some out, and take it to the steward of the feast." So they took it. (John 2:1–8)

Surely the Lord could have turned the very air into wine for the guests there. It may have been an even more impressive feat, in fact, if He had created the wine from nothing. But here's the thing: He didn't. He started with what they had.

He told them to fill their pitchers brimful, and then He started with that.

Andrew Kern often reminds us that as teachers we are saying "imitate me," whether or not we are worthy of imitation, and whether or not we want to be imitated. Cultivating intellectual growth, nurturing our creativity, diving into good books, learning new skills, working refreshment into a busy routine—that is how we fill our pitchers brimful of water.

We fill up when we read a good book, take a long hike, listen and learn, and connect with others. While we're doing it, it doesn't really feel like much. It certainly doesn't feel like wine. But it doesn't really matter, because He never asked us for wine. All He needs is our pitcher of water.

There are many ways to do this, and it's probably going to look slightly different for all of us.

Here Are a Few Ways to Intentionally Fill Your Own Pitcher Brimful

Choose a literary mentor.

I often choose one particular literary mentor to guide my reading through a year. Last year mine was Chesterton. Of course, it will always be Chesterton, at least a little, but this year I'm ready to sit at someone else's feet, and I'm soaking up wisdom and insight from Elizabeth Goudge.

We can choose to read any good books, of course, but I find it helpful to choose one particular author each year to focus on. I usually choose a few of his or her books and scatter them throughout my own reading during the year, paying special attention to what they can teach me about living fully and well. As I near the end of a year, I'll begin to ask friends I look up to and trust which author has fed and nourished their souls. Which books have had the most transformative impact on their lives? If I hear a particular author mentioned a few times by different people, I know I've got a potential mentor to look up to.

I tend to choose literary mentors who are somewhat prolific so that I can choose just a couple of titles from their literary buffets. Just a few ideas to choose from: C.S. Lewis, G.K. Chesterton, Elizabeth Goudge, Flannery O'Connor, Wendell Berry, P.G. Wodehouse, J.R.R. Tolkien, Charlotte Mason, Jane Austen, William Shakespeare, Alfred Tennyson, Anthony Esolen, James Sire, Dorothy Sayers, T.S. Eliot—just pick one author, steep yourself in his or her writing, and see what impact that has on your reading and on your living.

Take a class.

We have a unique opportunity to use technology to connect with the great thinkers of our own age. Lucky for us, many of these people are taking the time to share their insights and wisdom through online classes and courses.

At Classical Academic Press, Dr. Christopher Perrin teaches a seminar for teachers and homeschool moms to infuse their learning environment with *scholé*—deep and restful learning (see ScholeAcademy.com). The CiRCE apprenticeship (see CirceInstitute.org) offers personal tutoring and training for teachers who want to make the transformation of souls and the shaping of the habits of mind the utmost priority in their teaching. Look around for opportunities to learn from the great thinkers of our own time, to stand on the shoulders of giants while keeping your feet firmly planted on the reality of today.

If we were teachers in a school, we would be cultivating our professional development because that is what teachers do. So why not invest in ourselves similarly, as teachers within our homes? It takes a subtle paradigm shift to realize that part of our homeschool budget (of both time and money) ought to be set aside for the nurturing of our abilities as teachers of students we have been charged with. Make your own learning and growing a priority, and watch how that impacts the life of your homeschool.

Keep a commonplace book.

Commonplace books aren't anything new. For centuries, these personal collections have played a significant role in the way scholars read, learn, and remember. They paint a beautiful picture of an individual's growth over time—of his or her personal journey of learning and growing.

When I'm reading and I run across a beautiful passage or something that moves me, I copy it into my commonplace. Sometimes I draw a line down the middle of each paper and copy the passage on the left and my response to that passage on the right. Other times I just copy down the passage. Writing it out by hand helps the passage become a part of me somehow. It's a little hard to explain, but if you try it, you'll know what I mean.

In my commonplace book, I jot down snippets, quotes, and stanzas. They can be words from a novel, from a poem, from a picture book, from the side of a cereal box. Anything I read that causes me to pause and read again—to stop and savor the words or ponder the message—it all belongs in my book. This is the heart of my commonplace and what really makes it a treasure.

I tend to go in spurts with my commonplace, feverishly writing down everything that strikes me or comes to mind in one season, then ignoring it and allowing it to collect dust in the next. It's natural—the waxing and waning of enthusiasm and desire to grow, think, and reflect. I have noticed, however, that my ability to read hard books, think deep thoughts, and discern and cull insight, is a direct reflection on how often I'm using my commonplace.

If you need some practical help getting started, we have a simple Beginner's Guide to the Commonplace Book workshop available at amongstlovelythings.com/commonplace-book.

Copy a Scripture passage by hand.

Andrew Pudewa from the Institute for Excellence in Writing (IEW. com) once told me that he was changed by his attempts to copy out the first chapter of John by hand. I assign my children copywork on a regular basis, but somehow it had not occurred to me that I ought to try it myself.

But of course I should! That's slow contemplation. It's soul soaking. It's filling the pitcher to overflowing. When I write the passage down, I notice things I skip over when I'm reading it over as I've done a hundred times before. It doesn't have to be John, of course, but the poetic beauty of this gospel makes it a real treat to copy down.

Choose any bit of Scripture—short or long. Spend just five minutes each day copying a bit of it down. Each day, read over what you've written and add a few more sentences, and see how this practice transforms you little by little.

Start a Scholé Sisters Group.

A Scholé Sisters group is a small gathering of women who desire to cultivate restful learning in their own personal lives. Deciding to devote yourself to *scholé*—to cultivating truth, goodness, and beauty—not just in your kids, but in yourself—is deciding to be fully human.

A like-minded group of friends, seeking truth together and enjoying one another's companionship can go a long way toward helping the tired, busy homeschooling mother regain a sense of peace and live out this concept of *scholé*. I know of many women who gather on a monthly or quarterly basis to talk about books, sip wine, and encounter big ideas together through leisurely conversation. It's a beautiful thing, and one that we would do well to imitate whenever possible.

We are wearied by checking off our to-do lists, only to draw up a whole new list the next day. We are wells, offering of ourselves by the bucketful, but we must refill the well. Doing that with like-minded friends helps us live out the call to develop ourselves as fully as we can and help others do the same.

When I'm excited about something new I've learned, I really want to connect with someone about it. This is, I think, especially important when you decide to take on some weighty intellectual thinking. Thinking is the art of asking questions, and that's just not done terribly well in a vacuum. We were made for community!

I know the challenge of carving out time to nourish your heart and mind. Of course there are many things that matter and that are worth making time for—our prayer lives, nurturing our marriages, spending time lavishly on our kids—all of those are things that matter. But so are reading, discussing, asking questions, and cultivating your intellect—they are all part of being fully human, and they matter too. I wonder how good a job we can do at nurturing the beautiful humanity in our children if we are disengaged so thoroughly from our own.

If teaching is the art of imitation, then we ought to make ourselves worthy of imitation. By our very nature, as mothers we are saying "imitate me." Cultivating intellectual growth, nurturing your creative side, diving into good books, learning a new skill, working refreshment into your busy routine—that is what *scholé* is all about. Forming a small group of women who meet on a regular basis to do it together and to encourage one another along the way is what sisterhood is all about.

When we meet regularly with other women to read a classic, do an hour of nature study, or learn to paint with watercolors, we are demonstrating with our very lives that the world is worth learning about, our minds are worth cultivating, and people are worth loving. We model delight in learning something new, and we demonstrate what it looks like to find like-minded peers to encourage and to be encouraged by. Isn't this the very thing we long for our children to do?

Sometimes getting out for an evening of fellowship with other women is difficult, however. Nursing infants, a husband with a hectic work schedule, sick children, and other family dynamics don't always allow us to meet, as much as we would love for it to be a part of our reality.

Meetings don't have to be extravagant, frequent, or expensive, though. It can be a simple regular phone call with a friend to discuss *The Great Gatsby*. It can be a meeting once a month in someone's home with candles and calm music to discuss *Hamlet*. It can be meeting at a state park or wildlife refuge one Saturday morning a month to learn the names of a few local trees. A class at the art studio to learn the basics of watercolor. A gathering at your house every other month to have a nice breakfast and read poetry. It can be a writing club, a knitting club, a book club, a cooking club.

Scholé is the art of restful, deep, and meaningful learning. Sisterhood is the art of connecting with the women God has placed in our lives.

So what about you? How will you fill your pitcher? If what we want from our students is the ability to contemplate, behold, and be transformed by truth, beauty, and goodness, we would do well to live that out ourselves.

Afterword

"School is not about school," Andrew Kern says. "Homeschooling is not about school. It's about pursuing wisdom; it's about becoming virtuous beings; it's about soul transformation."[1]

We don't view our children as products coming off a factory line—no, we view them as human beings made in the image and likeness of God. We seek to cultivate and nourish their souls on truth, goodness, and beauty by means of the arts they study with us in our homes.

Given this lofty aim, why do we care so much if we have checked all the boxes we meant to check when we started the school year? How important is it really what grade level your child reads at? He reads as well as he can, so continue to work diligently at it. This is one of the great benefits of home-schooling—we don't have to follow a prescribed pace for a class of thirty students. In a homeschool setting, when we are seeking to cultivate wisdom in our children, it doesn't matter how far we get in the "6th grade" math book. Rather, we encounter math every day and work diligently at it. The only time we really care about how our children compare to other children is when we're giving in to our own vanity, when we're worrying about what other people think of us and the way we homeschool.

You are where you are (which is likely to be exactly where God wants you). So work hard every day. Value academic work because nurturing the intellect is part of what makes us fully human, but don't elevate it beyond its place. There are relationships to cultivate, books to read, oceans to swim in, forts to build, toilets to scrub, bills to pay, paintings to create, dinners to make. This is why we homeschool—because we want to engage in a full-to-bursting life.

Do we really think we need the perfect math curriculum? The best lineup of books we can find? Do we think God *needs* that to work

---

1. Andrew Kern, "Teaching from a State of Rest (Part 3)," *Videos*, CiRCE Institute, February 2014, available at https://www.circeinstitute.org/node/2808.

through us? I'm pretty sure if we just offer up our simple best and do it without fretting or becoming anxious over many things, then God can bless that a thousandfold. And I believe He will.

Of course we are going to research curriculum. We are going to assess our students and note their progress (and maybe judiciously use a checklist from time to time!). Of course we are going to think carefully about how we go about this incredibly important task of raising our students up to love truth, goodness, and beauty. God does indeed want our all as we take on this supremely high task to which we have been called.

We make a grave mistake when we think that the success of our homeschool hinges on whether or not we can pull together the ideal curriculum or read the best books or teach our children the nuances of long division before they're twelve. A further mistake: We make the entire enterprise all about ourselves.

Without a doubt, God loves to do great things in the lives of children through the toil of their hardworking, ever-loving mothers. But He works through the consecrated toil of moms who are submitted to His Son and who work with divine energy not their own (see Colossians 1:28–29). God certainly does not want us to labor on our own, burning the candle at both ends, wearing out our souls and spending sleepless nights tossing and turning with worry about whether or not we are doing a good enough job.

God doesn't need you. *But He wants to work through you.*

We need to show up in trust, leaning not on our own understanding and strength, and get our marching orders for the day. We need to relieve ourselves of the burden we feel to do this work perfectly, to not mess up. We should confidently go into our day, thinking to ourselves, "Well, I'm going to make some mistakes today. Thank God for grace, His presence, and His promise to work through me!" and give it our all anyway. We know that God will use our mistakes just as thoroughly as He uses our successes, and so we rest in that.

One of my favorite priests, Father John Riccardo of Detroit, Michigan, tells us, "The gospel isn't about rolling up our sleeves and trying harder. The gospel is about tapping into His power."

Take a deep breath, mama. This isn't as dependent on you as you think it is. Give God your "Here I am. Use me." Let Him carry the burden.

The God who turned water into wine can take our smallest efforts and weave them into a glorious tapestry for His delight. I pray that the peace of God will guard your heart and your mind in Christ Jesus.

Resources

Teaching from Rest Companion Journal and *Audio Collection*

The *Teaching from Rest Companion Journal* is available as a printable PDF file to help you start digging in to how you can make the principles in this book come to life in your home. Get inspired by the people who inspired me! The *Teaching from Rest Audio Companion* is a collection of conversations between myself and the educators and mentors I admire. The audio companion is delivered as a set of four MP3 downloads.

Andrew Kern:

Teach from a State of What?!

Dr. Christopher Perrin:

Scholé: Changing the Way We Think about School

Brandy Vencel:

Let's Get Real: Mothering from a State of Rest

Cindy Rollins:

If I Knew Then What I Know Now

Recommended Resources

Scholé Sisters

A space to nourish your soul, cultivate your intellect, and help you become worthy of imitation. Mothering is the art of being imitated, and Scholé Sisters provides the inspiration and the tools you need to harness truth, beauty, and goodness in yourself and in your kids. If you need help getting a Scholé Sisters Group off the ground, you can find a free guide written by my own little group of Scholé Sisters at amongstlovelythings.com/schole-ebook.

Scholé Groups

Scholé Groups are homeschooling communities infused with and guided by the ideal of restful learning, or *scholé*. If you would like to organize or join a Scholé Group, visit ScholeGroups.com.

Scholé Academy

Scholé Academy is an online academy that offers live, teacher-led online courses for homeschooling families, and seeks to embody the ideals of restful learning online. You can learn more at ScholeAcademy.com.

Leisure: The Basis of Culture by Josef Pieper

The official guide on what it really means to rest and be renewed. Pieper tips our understanding of the word "leisure" on its head in this landmark book. I highly recommend it.

In Conversation with God series by Francis Fernandez

This collection of meditations for the daily readings of the Church is by far the best I've seen. Many reflections pair scriptural reflections with the wise and comforting words of St. Josemaría Escrivá.

Holiness for Housewives and Other Working Women **by Hubert Van Zeller**

I reread this book by Hubert Van Zeller every year. If you need a short book to help you sanctify the ordinary and find God in your here and now, get your hands on this. You'll be glad you did!

Holy Is the Day: Living in the Gift of the Present **by Carolyn Weber**

A spiritual memoir that will help you see the beautiful holiness all around you. Weber's lyrical writing style and deep insights captivated and inspired me.

Teaching from a State of Rest **video series by Andrew Kern of the CiRCE Institute**

http://circeinstitute.org/video

I hope every homeschooling mom gets a chance to see this collection of Andrew Kern's presentation on teaching from a state of rest. I recommend a little cheat: Skip to video three, click your cursor on 28:08, and watch the last ten minutes of the third video. Then, when you are thoroughly encouraged and motivated, start at the very beginning and watch the whole series.

Recovering Leisure in Education

http://tinyurl.com/o68qp32

This set of videos by Dr. Christopher Perrin explores the concept of *scholé*.

The Liturgical Classroom and Virtue Formation

http://tinyurl.com/on65pkn

How you teach is more important than what you teach, and no one says that better than Jenny Rallens in this video. Jenny is revolutionizing the way I think about learning.

Bibliography

Aquinas, Thomas. "Prayer Before Study." Aquinas College. Last modified April 29, 2013. http://www.aquinascollege.edu/prayer-before-study-exams-spring-2013/.

Augustine. *Confessions*. Translated by R.S. Pine-Coffin. New York: Penguin, 1983.

Barnhill, Pam. *Plan Your Year: Homeschool Planning with Purpose and Peace*. Dothan, AL: Amazon Digital Services, 2014.

Bean, Danielle, and Elizabeth Foss. *Small Steps for Catholic Moms: Your Daily Call to Think, Pray, and Act*. Notre Dame, IL: Ave Maria Press, 2013.

Caldecott, Stratford. *Beauty in the Word: Rethinking the Foundations of Education*. Tacoma, WA: Angelico Press, 2012.

Carney, Julia A. Fletcher. "Little Things." In *Famous Poems from Bygone Days*, edited by Martin Gardner, 36. Mineola, NY: Dover Publications, 1995.

Chesterton, G.K. *Orthodoxy*. Lexington, KY: Ortho Publishing, 2014.

Clark, Kevin, and Ravi Scott Jain. *The Liberal Arts Tradition: A Philosophy of Christian Classical Education*. Camp Hill, PA: Classical Academic Press, 2013.

DeYoung, Kevin. *Crazy Busy: A (Mercifully) Short Book about a (Really) Big Problem*. Wheaton, IL: Crossway, 2013.

Fernandez, Francis. *In Conversation with God*. 6 vols. London: Scepter, 2010.

Kempis, Thomas à. *The Imitation of Christ*. Peabody, MA: Hendrickson Christian Classics, 2004.

Kern, Andrew. "Forging a Likeness." *CiRCE Magazine*, November 2013: 6.

———. "Teaching from a State of Rest (Part 3)." *Videos*. CiRCE Institute. February 2014. https://www.circeinstitute.org/node/2808.

Lewis, C.S. *Letters of C.S. Lewis*. Edited by W.H. Lewis. New York: Mariner Books, 2003.

———. *Mere Christianity*. San Francisco: HarperSanFrancisco, 2001.

———. *The Screwtape Letters*. San Francisco: HarperSanFrancisco, 2001.

———. *The Weight of Glory*. New York: HarperOne, 2009.

Macaulay, Susan Schaeffer. *For the Children's Sake: Foundations of Education for Home and School*. Wheaton, IL: Crossway, 2009.

Mason, Charlotte M. *A Philosophy of Education*. Wheaton, IL: Tyndale House, 1989.

Perrin, Christopher. "Learning and Leisure: Developing a School of Scholé." *Inside Classical Education* (blog), November 24, 2010. http://insideclassicaled.com/?p=295.

———. "*Multum Non Multa.*" *About Dr. Christopher Perrin*. Classical Academic Press. February 7, 2014. http://classicalacademicpress.com/about-dr-christopher-perrin/.

Pieper, Josef. *Leisure: The Basis of Culture*. San Francisco: Ignatius Press, 2009.

Plutarch. "On Listening." In *Essays*, translated by Robin H. Waterfield, edited by Ian Kidd, 19–50. London: Penguin Classics, 1993.

Rollins, Cindy. "What Is Morning Time and Why Bother?" *Morning Time Moms*. August 5, 2014. http://www.ordo-amoris.com/2014/08/what-is-morning-time-and-why-bother.html.

Swenson, Richard A. *Margin: Restoring Emotional, Physical, Financial, and Time Reserves to Overloaded Lives*. Colorado Springs, CO: NavPress, 1992.

Van Zeller, Hubert. *Holiness for Housewives and Other Working Women*. Manchester, NH: Sophia Institute Press, 1997.

Vencel, Brandy. "Secrets from Charlotte Mason on Scheduling for Peace." *AfterThoughts* (blog). Accessed June 11, 2015. Available at http://after-thoughtsblog.net/2014/06/secrets-from-charlotte-mason-on.html.

Wilder, Laura Ingalls. *Laura Ingalls Wilder, Farm Journalist: Writings from the Ozarks*. Edited by Stephen W. Hines. Columbia: University of Missouri, 2007.

About the Author

Sarah Mackenzie is a smitten wife and a homeschooling mama of six (including twins!). When she isn't immersed in daily chaos and large-family life, she's writing about books, babies, and heaps of grace. Visit her online at amongstlovelythings.com or at ScholeSisters.com, where she serves as editor-in-chief of a community of moms seeking to model delight, nurture minds, and order loves. She also hosts the Read-Aloud Revival podcast and membership site, which can be found at readaloudrevival.com.

Connect with Sarah and her readers, get all the *Teaching from Rest* resources, and stay in touch by visiting classicalacademicpress.com or teachingfromrest.com.

Notes

Notes

CLASSICAL EDUCATION
BOOK SERIES

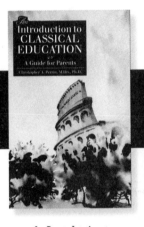

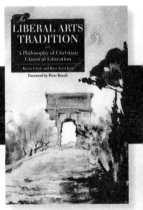

An Introduction to
Classical Education
A Guide for Parents

A Student's Guide to
Classical Education
One Student's K–12
Journey

The Liberal Arts
Tradition
A Philosophy of
Christian Classical
Education

CLASSICAL ACADEMIC PRESS.com
Classical Subjects Creatively Taught